I0636460

Classic Bottled Beers of the World

In the same series:

Classic Stout and Porter
Roger Protz
Classic Bourbon, Tennessee & Rye Whiskey
Jim Murray
Classic Irish Whiskey
Jim Murray
Classic Cocktails
Salvatore Calabrese
Classic Vodka
Nicholas Faith & Ian Wisniewski

Classic Bottled Beers of the World

Roger Protz

My thanks to all the brewers who responded to telephone calls, letters, faxes, and e-mails for information. Special thanks are due to Andrew Goodfellow, my editor at Prion, for his patience and forbearance. Never has such a kindness been shown before by a follower of Manchester United to a supporter of West Ham United!

First published in Great Britain in 1997 by PRION BOOKS
32-34 Gordon House Road London NW5 1LP

Editorial co-ordination by Lynn Bryan
Designed by Jill Plank

A CIP catalogue record for this book is available from the British Library.
ISBN 1-85375-219-3

Printed in Hong Kong

Contents

HOW BEER IS BREWED

ALL BEERS ARE THE RESULT OF UNLOCKING SUGARS IN MALTED BARLEY AND OTHER CEREALS, BOILING THE SWEET SOLUTION WITH HOPS FOR BITTERNESS AND AROMA AND THEN FERMENTING THE LIQUID WITH SPECIAL STRAINS OF BREWER'S YEAST.

The finest brewing grain is pale barley malt. This has the highest amount of natural enzymes to turn starch into sugar during the mashing stage.

Ale, a style of beer most prevalent in Britain and Belgium and with growing support among small producers in the United States, is brewed by the top or warm fermentation method (so named because ale yeasts tend to rise to the top of the fermenting beer). Using this process, barley malt – pale is often blended with darker crystal and occasionally black, chocolate and roasted versions – is mixed with pure hot water in a mash tun. The thick porridge stands for a few hours while enzymes convert starch to sugar. Wort, the resultant sweet liquid, is boiled for between one and one and a half hours with hops. Ale hops, mainly grown in Britain, are

Opposite
Burnished copper brew kettles at Spendrup's brewery near Stockholm, Sweden, where malt and hops add flavour and aroma to beer.
Below
Barley fields provide the grain that becomes malt, described by brewers as "the soul of beer".

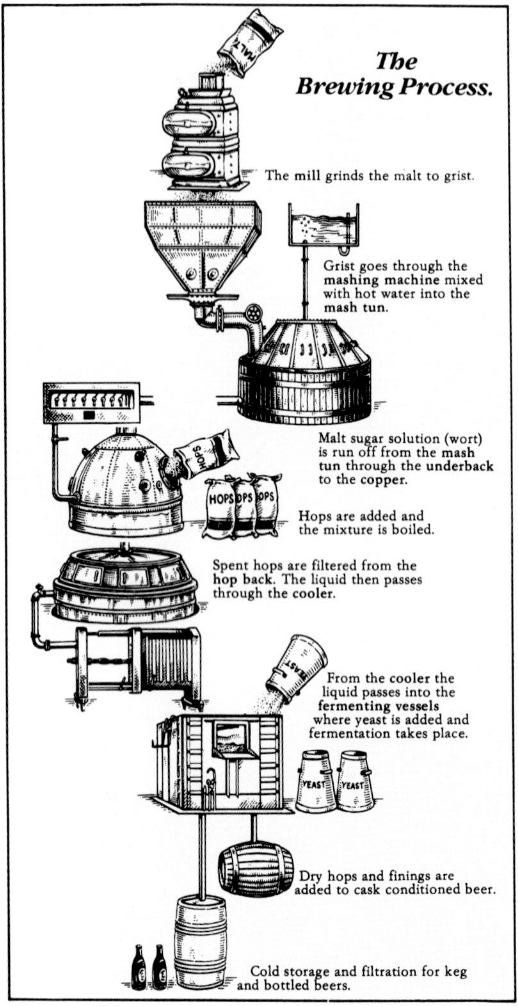

The Brewing Process.

MALT

The **mill** grinds the malt to grist.

Grist goes through the **mashing machine** mixed with hot water into the **mash tun**.

Malt sugar solution (wort) is run off from the **mash tun** through the **underback** to the **copper**.

HOPS

HOPS

Hops are added and the mixture is boiled.

Spent hops are filtered from the **hop back**. The liquid then passes through the **cooler**.

YEAST

From the **cooler** the liquid passes into the **fermenting vessels** where yeast is added and fermentation takes place.

YEAST YEAST

Dry hops and finings are added to cask conditioned beer.

Cold storage and filtration for keg and bottled beers.

pollinated and seeded, and give earthy, spicy, peppery and citric fruit aromas and flavours to beer and act as anti-bacterial preservatives. The hopped wort is then fermented for about a week. Ale yeast creates a thick head on top of the liquid and, as well as converting sugar to alcohol, gives a house style to a beer – often a rich fruitiness. After fermentation, ale may be filtered and pasteurized. The finest versions, known as "real ale" in Britain, undergo a natural secondary fermentation.

Opposite
Grist to the mill. A flow chart from Eldridge Pope's Thomas Hardy Brewery in Dorchester, England, showing the stages of the ale brewing process.

Lager brewing, known as bottom or cold fermentation because lager yeast works at the bottom of the vessel, is a result of the 19th-century industrial revolution. Ice-making machines let brewers ferment and store (lager is the German word for store) at temperatures much lower than those used in ale brewing. After mashing and boiling (using seedless hops with restrained aromas and flavours) primary fermentation is followed by several weeks and even months at low temperatures. This slow secondary fermentation purges it of unwanted flavours, producing clean and refreshing beers.

A third and ancient method used in Belgium produces members of the lambic and gueuze family. The beers, a blend of malted barley and wheat with hops that have been aged to avoid too much bitterness, are left open to the air to ferment spontaneously with wild yeasts and are stored in wooden casks where micro-organisms attack the sugars. Cherries and raspberries can be added to make fruit beers.

The Language of Beer

ABV Alcohol by volume, the measure of strength.

Adjuncts Additional cereals to barley malt used in the mashing process, such as maize, rice or wheat.

Ale Beer brewed by top fermentation and warm conditioning.

Alpha acid Bittering agent in the hop plant.

Altbier Literally "old beer", a German ale associated with the city of Düsseldorf.

Barley wine Strong ale; strongest beer in an English brewery.

Berliner Weisse A wheat beer of Berlin brewed with a lactic yeast culture that adds tart sourness.

Bière de garde A northern French ale originally brewed for storing: a "beer to keep".

Bitter The classic English draught version of pale ale.

Bock A strong German lager brewed on a seasonal basis, often during Lent. Stronger versions are known as Doppelbock. "Bok" in Dutch.

Bottle-conditioned Ale that undergoes a secondary fermentation in the bottle and throws a yeast sediment.

Burtonize Addition of gypsum salts to brewing liquor to replicate the hard waters of Burton-on-Trent.

Caramalt Barley malt kilned to a darker colour than pale, similar to English crystal malt.

Caramel Roasted sugar added to give colour and flavour.

Carbon dioxide Gas produced during fermentation.

Cask Container for draught beer.

Cask-conditioned Draught beer that undergoes a secondary fermentation in the cask.

Decoction Mashing system used mainly in lager brewing. Portions of the mash are transferred between vessels and heated to a higher temperature.

Dortmunder The style of lager beer associated with the German city Dortmund. Shortened to Dort.

Dunkel German dark lager beer.

Eisbock Bavaria lager beer in which the water in the beer is frozen, increasing the alcoholic strength.

Export A premium ale or lager that was once sold outside its home territory.

Hefe German word for yeast. *Mit-Hefe* indicates an unfiltered beer: usually a Bavarian wheat beer.

Helles or Hell Bavarian pale lager.

India Pale Ale Classic English pale beer made famous in Burton-on-Trent for export to the colonies.

Infusion One vessel mashing system used in ale brewing.

Kölsch Golden top-fermented beer made in Cologne.

Kräusen Addition of some partially fermented wort to lager beer to encourage a second fermentation.

Lager From the German word for storage.

Lambic Belgian beer fermented by wild yeast. Faro is a sweetened version; Gueuze is a blend of lambics; Kriek is lambic with cherries, and Frambozen has the addition of raspberries.

Lauter tun Vessel used during the mashing process to clarify the wort.

Maibock Strong German beer brewed in Spring.

Märzen Bavarian lager beer brewed in March and stored until the Munich Oktoberfest.

Mild English term for a lightly hopped ale, brewed with dark malt. Is brown ale when bottled.

Münchener Classic lager beer of Munich.

Munich malt Barley malt cured to give a burnished gold colour to beer.

Old ale Historically, an English ale stored for a year or more. Also called "stale", it was a constituent of early Porters. Either a seasonal or a strong ale.

Pale Ale Less heavily hopped version of India Pale Ale. Now the bottled version of Bitter in England.

Pilsner Lager beer originating in Pilsen. Also spelt Pilsener or Pils. Much-abused term that now indicates a brewery's premium lager.

Porter Dark, heavily hopped beer developed in London in the 18th century.

Rauchbier Bavarian specialty made from malt smoked over a wood fire.

Reinheitsgebot Bavarian "Pure Beer Pledge" dating from 1516 that permits only malted cereals, hops, yeast and water in beer.

Saison Artisan beers from French-speaking Belgium, originally seasonal ales.

Schwarzbier German for black beer, a dark lager brewed in Bavaria and Thuringia.

Scotch Strong malty ale brewed originally in Scotland, exported to England and the Low Countries.

Steam beer San Francisco speciality, a hybrid beer brewed at ale temperatures but with a lager yeast.

Stout Historically, the strongest or stoutest version of Porter. Now a style in its own right.

Trappist Bottle-conditioned ales brewed by monks in Belgium and the Netherlands.

Urquell German for "original source". Word added to Pilsener in Pilsen to stress it was the first beer of the style.

Urtyp German for original, often added to name of company's founding beer.

Vienna Austrian style of lager now hard to find, brewed with Vienna Red amber malt .

Wheat/White beer *Weisse* or *weizen* in German, *blanche* or *wit* in French and Flemish: beer brewed from blend of wheat and barley malt.

Wort Sugary extract resulting from mashing process.

Bottled History

Bottled beer was a luxury until the 19th century industrial revolution turned glass manufacture into a large-scale commercial enterprise. Until the beginning of the 17th century beer that wasn't run into casks was consumed from bottles made from leather or earthenware: there are still a few English pubs called The Old Leather Bottle to mark the fact. It is thought that the term "bootlegger" comes from the habit of concealing a flat leather bottle of beer or strong spirits in a jackboot.

According to English essayist Izaak Walton, Dr Alexander Nowell, Dean of St Paul's Cathedral in London from 1560 to 1602, discovered the virtues of bottled beer when he left a corked bottle by a river bank after a day's fishing. When he returned a few days later he discovered "not a bottle but a gun, so great was the sound of the opening thereof". Clearly the beer had been bottled with some yeast and unfermented sugars and had built up a high level of carbon dioxide. It is not known whether this famous bottle was made from glass or stoneware: the latter remained popular until well into the 19th century.

Glass manufacture aided brewers who were engaged in the export market. Beer survived long sea journeys better in bottle than in cask: casked beer could become contaminated and sailors were dab hands at helping themselves to draught beer. Bottles could be re-used and were

Above
The Welsh brewer Felinfoel, which had close links to the tin-plate industry, introduced canned beer in the 1930s, and is thought to be the first brewery to have done so.

light and easy to handle. At first they were shaped like bulbous flagons and were corked. When hand-blown glass was replaced by moulding machines, beer bottles adopted the shape of a Bordeaux wine bottle, which could be stored horizontally. Beer was forced into bottles by compressed air and corks were soon replaced by screw stoppers or crown caps.

Bottled beer made slow headway in England as a result of heavy tax on glass. This was only lifted late in the 19th century as brewers were faced by competition from imported European lager beer. Pale ale not only met this threat head-on in bottle but became a cult drink for

FORDHAM'S
Noted
ASHWELL BREWERY HERTS
BOTTLED
BY THE
BREWERS.
E.K.&H. FORDHAM
PALE ALE
ASHWELL, HERTS
IMPERIAL PINTS
E.K.&H. FORDHAM
XXXX STOUT
ASHWELL, HERTS
IMPERIAL PINTS
BEST PALE ALE
IMP PINTS
4/-
PER DOZEN
HALF PINTS
2/3
PER DOZEN
GOLD MEDAL STOUT
IMP PINTS
4/-
PER DOZEN
HALF PINTS
2/3
PER DOZEN
XX STOUT 3/- PER DOZEN
DINNER ALE
3/-
PER DOZEN.
LIGHT
BITTER ALE 2/6 PER DOZEN

the rising middle class who preferred to drink at home rather than in "common" pubs. They appreciated the clarity and sparkle of bottled pale ale and left the working classes to drink murky brown ales and porters in pubs. The London brewer Whitbread delivered bottled beer to customers' doors. Advertising showed elegant, upper-class ladies enjoying a glass of Whitbread Pale Ale after a round of golf.

Initially, bottled beer contained yeast and underwent a secondary fermentation but the ale brewers soon followed in the footsteps of the lager manufacturers and filtered and chilled their ales. Early in the 20th century many brewers also pasteurized bottled beers. As Louis Pasteur had developed his method to kill bacteria in wine and specifically did not recommend it for the delicate flavours of beer, it is remarkable that it is still in use, often giving a cooked vegetable flavour to beer. As such major brewers as Brand and Grolsch in the Netherlands do not pasteurize their lagers, it is odd that the system still has such a hold when modern cold filtration methods abound.

With the exception of Great Britain, where 70 per cent of beer is drunk on draught, most beer comes in bottled form. The can has made substantial inroads into bottled sales but it is an unappealing container, gives a "tinny" flavour to beer and most craft brewers avoid it. The finest bottled beers are those allowed to mature on their yeast.

Opposite
The long-defunct Fordham's brewery in Hertfordshire, England was typical of British brewers in the early part of the 20th century, offering their draught beers in bottled versions, containing an "imperial pint" and closed with a screw stopper.

BELGIUM

Belgium is the most fascinating of beer countries. There are beers with an ancestry that pre-dates 19th-century lagering techniques. They recall the time before the hop plant was used in beer making and when brewers allowed wild air-borne yeasts to be fermentation agents.

Drinkers may call for a lambic, gueuze, kriek or framboise from the family of spontaneous-fermentation beers; a "white" wheat beer; a Trappist ale made by monks; a sour red beer or an old brown ale. Aside from the lambic family, which form their own idiosyncratic style, the speciality beers of Belgium are top-fermenting ales. Many of them come in bottle-conditioned form, maturing on a natural sediment of yeast: these beers will improve with age.

Trappist ales have attracted much attention in recent years. Five of the six surviving Trappist monk breweries are in Belgium (the sixth is located in neighbouring Netherlands). Justly, God and Mammon have joined forces to allow the secular world to enjoy the liquid fruit of the monks' work.

Trappist ales are beers of great complexity and depth. As these are produced in both French and Flemish-speaking areas, they manage to bridge the gap between the cultural and linguistic communities in Belgium. However, the deserved fame of the monks' ales should not allow them totally to overshadow the other fine beers of the country, especially

Opposite
The elegant entrance to the Rochefort Trappist monastery at St Remy, one of five breweries run by monks in Belgium.

those from Wallonia where brewers dedicated to saisons and other distinctive styles feel they play second fiddle to the better-known products of the Flemish areas.

LAMBIC & GUEUZE

CANTILLON GUEUZE, ROSÉ DE GAMBRINUS AND KRIEK

Jean-Pierre Van Roy is arguably the greatest of the small, dedicated band of lambic, gueuze (gueuze being a blend of lambics) and fruit beer producers in Belgium. Lambic is such a bucolic beer style, with its roots in the rural landscape and gambolling peasants of the paintings of the Bruegels, that it is something of a shock to find Cantillon in the back streets of a district of Brussels best known for its passion for soccer. But Brussels lies in the valley of the River Senne or Zenne, where the particular strains of wild yeasts in the air – identified at the brewing school in the University of Leuven as *Brettanomyces bruxellensis* and *lambicus* – produce a beer style protected by Belgian law and a European Union ordinance.

Opposite
Cantillon is the classic producer of lambic and gueuze beers, made by spontaneous fermentation. Kriek is made with the addition of cherries while the Rosé de Gambrinus is a blend of cherries and raspberries.

And Van Roy is a descendant of a family of gueuze blenders who started work in the village of Lembeek, which is thought to have given its name to the style of lambic. The company moved to Anderlecht in 1900 and started to brew its own beers in the 1930s rather than just blend the lambics of other producers.

In the classic lambic style, the hopped wort is transferred to the shallow copper vessel or "cool ship" in the brewery attic under the roof. Windows are left open and tiles removed from the roof to encourage the air-borne yeasts to enter and attack the sugars in the wort. Once

fermentation is under way, the wort is moved to the dusty and dark alleys of large oak casks. Other yeasts and micro-flora in the air and the wood continue the fermentation. When cherries or raspberries are added to make fruit beers, they develop a further fermentation during which even the pips in the cherries are attacked.

Van Roy produces an occasional straight unblended lambic, the result of three years in wood and a further 12 months in bottle. His gueuze (5 per cent abv) is a blend of young and old lambic. It is a wonderfully complex beer, with a stunning tartness and acidity that puckers the mouth, some delicious cidery apple notes from the yeast and the wheat, and a dry, quenching, piquant fruit and sherry-like finish. *Kriek*, from the Flemish word for cherry, is the result of macerating the fruit in the oak tuns for six months. As the fruit turns to alcohol, the finished beer is far from sweet. The Burgundy-coloured 5 per cent brew has a pronounced dry cherry and almonds aroma (the nuttiness the result of the pips being eaten by the yeasts), tart fruit in the mouth and a long finish bursting with acids, tannins and fruit.

Rosé de Gambrinus (5 per cent) is a brilliant balance of cherry and raspberry fruit in the ratio of 25 per cent cherries and 75 per cent raspberries plus a touch of vanilla. Dry raspberries dominate aroma and palate with a hefty undertone of cherries. The pronounced sourness of the Gueuze and the Kriek is more refined in the Rosé. Van Roy brews only from late October to May but Cantillon is also a Gueuze Museum and is open to the public all year round.

Brasserie Cantillon, 56 Rue Gheude/Gheudestraat, Anderlecht, 1070 Brussels.

Left
Jean-Pierre Van Roy, passionate brewer of lambic at Cantillon, examines the quality of his work in the dusty brewhouse where the micro-organisms have a vital part to play in making beer.

BELLE-VUE SÉLÉCTION LAMBIC

The survival of the lambic and gueuze style was given an immeasurable boost in 1993 when Belle-Vue introduced a true, unsweetened gueuze. Belle-Vue was taken over by the giant Interbrew group in 1991, best known for Stella Artois and Jupiler Pils-style lagers. Belle-Vue, by the banks of the Zenne, produces 350,000 hectolitres a year (compared to Cantillon's 1,000), much of it sweet and sticky. But sweet beers are a dying market and the company, recognising that lambic and gueuze had become connoisseurs' drinks, made overtures to afiçionados with Séléction Lambic (5.2 per cent abv). Despite the name, the beer is a blended gueuze, unfiltered and bottle conditioned. It is a hazy copper colour, has an appealing aroma of roast chestnuts, is mouth-puckeringly sour with some spiciness and has a dry, fruity finish. The beer quickly won the seal of approval of the European Beer Consumers' Union.

Brasserie Belle-Vue, Rue Delaunoy 58, 1080 Brussels.

Old Brown

Liefmans Oud Bruin, Goudenband, Kriek and Frambozen

Oud Bruin – "Old Brown" – is the classic beer style of East Flanders and the waterside city of Oudenaarde. These brown ales are used in the famous Flemish beer dish, carbonade flamande or beef and onion stew. Liefmans, founded in 1679, grew in the 1970s and 1980s due to the enthusiasm and flair of Madame Rose Blancquaert, formerly the brewer's secretary, who ran the company after his death. The standard Oud Bruin (5 per cent abv) is made from a blend of Pilsner, Munich and Vienna malts and some roasted barley. Kentish

Whitbread Goldings Variety hops are used for bitterness with Czech and German varieties for aroma. The brewing liquor is soft. The beer is fermented in open vessels for seven days and is then matured for four months.

Goudenband (Gold Ribbon, 6 per cent) is a blend of Oud Bruin and a stronger ale that has matured for six to eight months. Following blending, the beer is given a dosage of yeast and matured in the brewery cellars for at least three months. This magnificently rich and complex bottle-conditioned beer has ripe raisin fruit and spicy hops on the aroma, chocolate and fruit in the mouth and a dry finish with a hint of sourness.

Above
Liefmans' Gold Ribbon is a blend of "old brown" ale and a stronger version matured for six to eight months, a method reminiscent of the one used for the early porters in England.

Once a year both cherries and raspberries are added to the unblended stronger beer, which then referments for up to two months. As a conventional, if multi-strain, brewer's yeast is used, Liefmans does not claim that its Kriek and Frambozen are lambics. The Kriek (7.1 per cent) has a deliciously dry and intense cherry fruitiness, while the 5.1 per cent Frambozen has a champagne sparkle in the glass plus a lilting aroma and palate of bitter-sweet fruit.

Brouwerij Liefmans, Aalstraat 200,
9700 Oudenaarde.

Opposite
Rodenbach was also influenced by English porter brewing. Its sour red beers are matured for many months in unlined oak vessels where natural micro-flora add a sour and lactic flavour to the beer.

SOUR RED BEER

RODENBACH, GRAND CRU AND ALEXANDER RODENBACH

The brewery on Spain Street produces the finest interpretation of the sour beers of West Flanders, the result of long maturation in unlined oak tuns. The sourness comes not from wild yeasts, as a conventional brewer's strain is used, but from the action of micro-organisms in the storage vessels.

The Rodenbachs came from near Koblenz in Germany. In 1820 Alexander Rodenbach, who was blind, took the courageous decision to open a small brewery. In the 1870s Eugene Rodenbach went on a fact-finding mission to England and returned determined to brew staled beers like English porters. The beer is made from a blend of pale malts, from both spring and winter barleys, and a darker Vienna malt that gives a reddish hue to the beer. Malt accounts for 80 per cent of the grist, the remainder coming from corn grits. Brewers' Gold and Kent Goldings hops are used, primarily for bitterness and as preservatives. A multi-strain top-fermenting yeast carries out primary fermentation for seven days, following which the wort has a second fermentation in metal tanks. Ageing takes place in ten halls of giant, red-hooped tuns. During the long rest in wood, lactobacilli add a sour, lactic quality to the beer. The regular Rodenbach (4.6 per cent abv) is a blend of a young, six week-old beer

and one that has been aged for at least 18 months. It has a sour, winey and woody aroma, is tart and quenching in the mouth with sherry-like fruit and a hint of quinine or iodine in the finish. Grand Cru is 5.2 per cent and is bottled straight from the tuns. It is bigger and more complex in every respect: oaky, tannic, sour and fruity. Both beers have some sugar added to take the extreme edge off the sourness and some drinkers added a dash of grenadine syrup. Alexander Rodenbach was made to celebrate the brewery's 150th anniversary. It is a version of Grand Cru with the addition of cherry essence and is perfect both as a pudding beer and for those who find the mainstream versions too tart and puckering.

Brouwerij Rodenbach, Spanjestraat 133, 8800 Roeselare.

WHITE BEER
HOEGAARDEN WHITE AND GRAND CRU.

Opposite *Hoegaarden has become a cult drink in the Low Countries and beyond. It has revived a style of brewing from the Middle Ages, when brewers used the spices and exotic fruits brought back by Dutch traders from the Indies to add superb aromas and flavours to their wheat beers.*

White or wheat beers, once an insignificant and almost ridiculed sideline, became cult drinks in Belgium and beyond in the 1980s. They were perceived by young people as being healthier than conventional beers and more characterful than mainstream Pils lagers. The pacesetter in the revival has been Hoegaarden. The rich soil of the Brabant region is ideal for growing cereals. Monks were brewing there from the 15th century and used the grain from the surrounding fields for their raw ingredients. Herbs and spices were added to blend with the malts and give tartness to the flavour. The wheat beers of Brabant became famous for the use of coriander and Curaçao orange peel.

But the style – known as white or *bière blanche* in French, *witbier* in Flemish – had been in sharp decline during the 20th century. Then in the 1960s Pierre Celis revived the style. He installed brewing equipment from another defunct plant and called his brewery De Kluis, The Cloister, in memory of the monks who had pioneered the style. Interbrew helped Celis after a serious fire in 1978 and eventually bought him out.

The 4.8 per cent abv bottle-conditioned beer is made from a 50-50 blend of malted barley and unmalted wheat with East Kent Goldings hops for aroma and Czech Saaz for light

Since 1445
NATURALLY CLOUDY · NON-FILTERED
BOTTLE CONDITIONED
Hoegaarden
White beer - Bière blanche
Since 1445
BELGIAN BEER
THE ORIGINAL WHITE BEER
33 cl
Hoegaarden

bitterness. Ground coriander seeds and orange peel are added during the copper boil. Following fermentation with an ale yeast strain, the beer is warm conditioned for up to a month and then primed with sugar and reseeded with yeast to encourage a second fermentation in bottle or keg. A young Hoegaarden has an appealing spicy nose with clear hints of the tart orange peel. It is quenching in the mouth with pronounced citric fruit, and the finish is bitter-sweet and clean. Grand Cru, 8.7 per cent, is not a stronger version of the White. It is a rendition again using coriander and orange, but made from barley malt without the addition of wheat. This rounded, warming beer has a ripe fruit cocktail aroma and palate balanced by spices and hops.

De Kluis Brouwerij van Hoegaarden, Stoopkensstraat 46, 3320 Hoegaarden.

TRAPPIST ALES

CHIMAY RED, WHITE & BLUE

Opposite
Chimay Première is a version of Red Cap in a large, Bordeaux-style bottle, a classic, fruity ale that can be laid down and matured to develop fuller flavours.

Once upon a time monasteries were at the heart of brewing throughout Europe. But dissolution and political victimization of monks have reduced monastic brewing to an historical fragment. In Austria and Germany a few monasteries still brew beer but the torch is held aloft most proudly by the Trappist monks of Belgium and the Netherlands, where Chimay is perhaps the best-known. The monks started to brew ale in the 1860s and were the first to use

the term Trappist Ale and sell their wares commercially after World War Two.

The local water is soft and acidic, which helps to emphasise the fruitiness of the ales. Belgian and French winter barleys are preferred for pale malt and caramalt, while hops are German Hallertauer and American Yakima

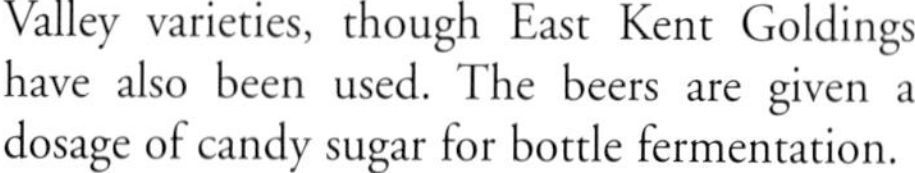

Valley varieties, though East Kent Goldings have also been used. The beers are given a dosage of candy sugar for bottle fermentation.

Chimay's three products are known by the colour of their caps. The original is Chimay Red (7 per cent abv), also known as Première in large, corked claret-style bottles. It has a blackcurrant fruit aroma balanced by spicy hops, a big malt and fruit palate and a long spicy, fruity finish. It can be drunk young but will improve with six months in bottle at a natural cellar temperature.

Chimay White (8 per cent) is also known as Cinq Cents in a larger corked bottle. White, a hazy peachy colour, is noticeably different to the Red and Blue, despite the influence of the house yeast. It is more fully attenuated – more sugars turned to alcohol – producing a drier beer with a pronounced spicy, peppery aroma and palate, and a fruitiness that is more restrained, citric and quenching.

The 9 per cent Blue (or Grande Réserve when in its larger bottle) is the most remarkable of the three ales and is ideal for laying down. Over the years it will develop greater depth of fruit and a pronounced port-wine character.

It has a booming blackcurrant and peppery hops aroma and palate, and a long, fruity, winey finish balanced by tart, spicy hops.

Abbaye de Notre-Dame de Scourmont, rue de la Trappe 294, 6438 Forges-les-Chimay.

ORVAL

Founded in 1070, Orval has been sacked, pillaged and burned over the ensuing centuries. It lay empty and desolate for many years until it was rebuilt and restored in the 1920s and 1930s. During the restoration, the monks decided to add a brewery to continue the long tradition of beer making.

The name is a corruption of *val d'or* – "golden valley". According to a quaint legend, a duchess of Tuscany came to visit Benedictine monks from Calabria, who had come from Italy to found a settlement in the Ardennes. As she sat by a spring in the grounds of the settlement her wedding ring fell into the water. She prayed that if the ring were restored to her she would found an abbey on the spot. At that moment, a trout rose to the surface with the gold ring in its mouth. The abbey was founded and the spring remains as the source for the brewery's liquor. A trout with a ring in its mouth is the trademark for the beer. Orval is unique among the Trappist breweries in making just one beer. It has a remarkable orange colour as a result of a blend of Beauce and Gatinais pale malts with caramalt. Candy sugar is added in the copper with German Hallertauer and East Kent Goldings hops. The beer has a powerful 40 units of bitterness and the hops give both an earthy and aromatic bouquet and great bitterness to the palate and finish. Primary fermentation uses a single strain

cultured yeast but a multi-strain of four or five yeasts is used for a secondary fermentation, during which time the beer rests on a bed of Goldings hops. One yeast strain is a wild one that gives a faint hint of lactic sourness to the finished beer.

Secondary fermentation lasts for six to seven weeks. The beer is then bottled with a dosage of priming sugar and the first single strain yeast, which start a third fermentation. The club-shaped bottles are held at warm temperature for two months before being released. The beer can be drunk young but will improve and deepen in character if it is stored for up to two years. It is declared at 5.2 to 5.7 per cent abv but will reach more than 6 per cent in bottle. Orval has an intense spicy, citric aroma and a deep and complex acidic palate and finish of gooseberry fruit and earthy hops. The dryness of the beer and its uncompromising bitterness makes it the best apéritif of all the Trappist ales.
Abbaye d'Orval, 6823 Villers-devant-Orval.

Opposite
Bottles of Orval, the sublime pale Trappist beer, maturing in a cool environment in the monastery deep in the Ardennes.

ROCHEFORT 6, 8 AND 10.

Rochefort is a pleasant Ardennes town with a spectacular choice of restaurants, bakeries and chocolate shops. The abbey is a few miles away, up a narrow, wooded country road. The community began life as a convent. When monks took over, they started to brew in 1595, using barley and hops grown in the grounds. Today, barley comes from France, Belgium and

the Netherlands in the form of pale Pilsner and darker Munich malts. Dark candy sugar is used in the copper, with Hallertauer and Styrian Goldings hops. The head brewer, Brother Antoine, presides over a superb brewhouse of gleaming and burnished copper mash tuns and coppers. Brother Antoine's beers are noticeably rich and fruity with a pronounced hint of malt loaf. The names 6, 8 and 10 come from an old system of measuring strength. Rochefort 6, with a red cap, is 7.5 per cent abv in modern terms. It has a red-brown colour and a deceptively mild, soft palate with sweet fruit and a hint of herbs. Rochefort 8 (9.2 per cent) is a big beer, copper-brown, with a rich fruity aroma and palate of raisins and dates.

The claret-coloured Rochefort 10 (11.3 per cent) has enormous depth, as its strength suggests. Gentle hops blend with dark fruit, nuts and chocolate. A two-strain yeast culture is used for primary and bottle conditioning and white sugar is used for bottle priming.
Abbaye de Notre-Dame de Saint-Rémy, 5580 Rochefort.

Opposite
Rochefort's ales are noticeably rich and fruity. Their labelling as 6, 8 and 10 comes from an old method of declaring strength.

WESTMALLE DUBBEL AND TRIPEL

Westmalle is one of two Trappist breweries in Flemish-speaking areas of Belgium. The abbey is north-east of the great city of Antwerp, on a tree-girt road in flat countryside. Most of the buildings at the brewery date from the early part of the 20th century, though the brewhouse was constructed later.

Their beers are denoted by the old designations of Double and Triple as a rough and ready indication of strength. The monks also brew a Single or *Enkel* for their own consumption, though this beer has occasionally been made available commercially.

The brotherly brewers choose summer barleys from France and Bavaria. Hops are German Tettnanger, Czech Saaz and Styrian Goldings. Candy sugar is added in the copper. The beers have a secondary fermentation in tanks – three weeks for Dubbel, five for Tripel – and are then primed with candy sugar and re-seeded with yeast for bottle conditioning.

Opposite
Monks at mash..brothers stirring the blend of malt and water in the first stage of the brewing process at the Westmalle brewery.

Dubbel also has some darker malt, giving the finished beer a russet colour, and a pronounced chocolate, nuts and ripe fruit character. Tripel (9 per cent abv) is the palest of all the Trappist beers. With just 13 units of colour, it looks just like a Pils but is a rich and unmistakable ale with a rounded malt aroma and palate balanced by spicy, perfumy hops, orange fruit and a herbal hint.

Abdij der Trappisten, Antwerpsesteenweg 396, 2390 Westmalle.

Westvleteren St Sixtus Green, Red, Blue & Abbot.

Westvleteren is the smallest of the Trappist breweries, based in West Flanders, close to the town of Ypres/Ieper and the hop fields of the Poperinge area. The full range of ales can be sampled opposite the abbey in the homely Café de Vrede.

The monks brew malt-accented beers. Their green-topped Double (4 per cent abv), a sweet yet spicy and refreshing ale, is produced mainly as the monks' table beer. Red (6.2 per cent) has a dark fruit and peppery hops character, the Blue (8.4 per cent) has an enormous attack of tart fruit and rich alcohol while the 10.6 Abbot has an explosion of fruit – raspberries and strawberries – and fat malt with a soft, silky and alluring creaminess.

Abdij Sint Sixtus, Donkerstaat 12, 8640 Westvleteren.

BELGIAN ALE

DE KONINCK

Opposite *The Moortgat Brewery at the turn of the century. It brewed brown beers long before the arrival of the classic golden ale, Duvel.*
Above *De Koninck, a king of beers, brewed in Antwerp's sole remaining commercial brewery.*

De Koninck means "the king" and it is a classic ale with an awesome complexity and dangerous drinkability. The brewery started life in 1833 as a humble brew-pub and beer garden and now has a modern brewhouse with the older one maintained as a museum. The 5 per cent abv beer is made from Pilsner and Vienna malts, the latter giving it its burnished copper colour. No sugars or cereal adjuncts are added. Unusually, just one hop variety, Saaz, is added at three stages during the copper boil. Fermentation is slow for an ale: eight days. The beer is then filtered. De Koninck pours with a dense, foaming head. The aroma is intensely hoppy and spicy. There is a toasty dark malt

roastiness in the mouth balanced by a gentle citric fruitiness from the house yeast. The beer has a long hoppy and fruity finish with a hint of spice.
Brouwerij De Koninck, Mechelsesteenweg 291, 2018 Antwerp 1.

DUVEL

Many people assume that Duvel is a French word and pronounce it *Duvelle.* But it is the Flemish for Devil and is pronounced as *Doo-vul,* with the emphasis on the first syllable. It is a golden ale, a bewitching beer of enormous depth and complexity and with a renowned fruitiness reminiscent of pears. The Moortgat brewery in Breendonk, north of Brussels, was founded in 1871 but Duvel did not appear

Above
Old labels for Duvel and Vedett, the latter a defunct beer from Moortgat.

until 1971. According to legend, the beer got its name when a brewery worker first tasted it and declared: "This is a devil of a beer!". Duvel has a complex brewing procedure. Two-row summer Belgian and French barleys are specially malted for Moortgat. Duvel has a colour rating of seven to eight, only fractionally higher than a Pilsner's. The beer is infusion mashed and the wort has a gravity of 1056 degrees. Saaz and Styrian Goldings hops are added to the copper boil in three stages, giving it 29 to 31 units of bitterness. Dextrose is added before primary fermentation to lift the gravity to 1066. Two strains of yeast are used for primary fermentation: the hopped wort is divided into two batches, each one attacked by a different yeast. Primary fermentation lasts for six days, followed by three days of secondary fermentation at cold temperature. The beer is cold conditioned for a month, filtered, and given a dose of dextrose and one of the original yeast strains. The gravity of the beer is again boosted, this time to 1073 degrees. The beer is bottled and stored for two weeks, when a third fermentation takes place. The result is a beer of 8.5 per cent abv. The aroma has a hint of Poire William. Aromatic hops and delicate fruit dominate the palate while the finish is perfumy. *Moortgat NV, Breendonkdorp 58, 2870 Breendonk.*

WALLONIAN SAISONS

DUPONT VIEILLE PROVISION

Brewers in the French-speaking areas of Belgium feel that, with the exception of the Trappist ales, their beers are lost in the giant shadow cast by the Flemish producers and are both overlooked and underrated. Yet Wallonia has one of the finest beer styles in the country: that of saison.

As the name implies, saison was originally a seasonal beer and has strong links with the *bière de garde* style of the Nord-Pas de Calais region of France across the border. Saisons are now usually brewed on a regular basis but their origins predate the industrial revolution, when it was not possible to brew in the summer months. Dupont's Vieille Provision – "Old Provision" – is the classic of the style.

It is brewed on a farm at Tourpes in flat Flanders countryside. The brewery was started in 1850 and has been owned by the Dupont family since the 1920s. Marc Rosier, grandson of the founders, with his sisters, is now in charge of the business and he is an articulate enthusiast for the saison style.

The farm has its own well which provides hard liquor for the charming, rustic and steam-filled brewhouse, where the mash tun doubles as the copper. Five to 6,000 hectolitres a year are produced, using pale and caramalts with East Kent Goldings and Styrian hops. Vieille Provision (6.5 per cent abv) has a deep, peppery

Above
Silly's Saison has helped to create greater interest in the beers from French-speaking Belgium.
Opposite
Selling beer is no laughing matter at Silly: old delivery trucks are on display in a small museum.

hoppiness from the Goldings, a hazy golden colour and a dense head when poured.

Dupont produces Avec Les Bons Voeux de la Brasserie, a 9.2 per cent Christmas ale, bursting with hops and citric fruit: the name gives you the best wishes of the brewery.

The company also brews under the Moinette label, named after Marc Rosier's farm. Moine means monk – the farm estate is thought to have once been an abbey. The two Little Monk beers are both 8.5 per cent and come in blonde and brune versions. The pale is hoppy and aromatic, the brown fruity and sweet.

The organic versions of Vieille Provision and Moinette are labelled *biologique*. The beers are sold in a café across the road.

Brasserie Dupont, rue Basse 5,
7904 Tourpes.

SAISON DE SILLY

The Saison style has achieved greater recognition in the English-speaking world due to the vigorous export policy of a brewery with a name that is perfectly sensible in French but highly amusing to British and Americans. The village of Silly and the brewery take their name from the local river, the Sil.

It is a farm brewery dating from the 1850s. The 5.4 per cent abv Saison Silly is brewed from French malts with Belgian caramalt for colour and English Goldings hops. In the small, cramped brewhouse the mash tun doubles as a hop back, with the wort returning to the tun for filtration after the copper boil.

Fermentation lasts for 15 days in small conical vessels, using a top-fermenting yeast strain. The beer is matured in tanks for two weeks and then filtered. The Saison is copper-coloured with peppery hops and winey fruit on the nose, dark fruit in the mouth and a dry, hoppy finish. Silly also brews pale and brown versions of a beer called Double Enghien (named after Enghien, a nearby village which once had its own brewery); a Silly Scotch; a superb 9.5 per cent Divine, an "artisanal" beer with a big peppery hops aroma, dark fruit and hops in the mouth and a bitter fruity finish. The bottle-conditioned 5 per cent Titje wheat beer has a lemon jelly aroma, tart citric fruit and spices in the mouth and a quenching finish.
Brasserie de Silly, Ville Basse A141,
7830 Silly.

WALLONIAN STRONG ALE
BUSH BEER

Opposite
Dubuisson brews the strongest ales in Belgium. the 12 per cent beer is in the style of an English barley wine. A darker and even fruitier version is made for the Christmas season.

At 12 per cent abv, Bush Beer is the strongest beer brewed regularly in Belgium. The brewery began life as a farm and still has a rustic feel to it even though it stands alongside the busy main road that runs from Mons to Lille in France. The attractive, green-shuttered buildings by the road act as administration offices for the brewery that dates back to 1769. The name of the single beer brand was anglicised to Bush (*buisson* means bush in French) as the result of the popularity of strong

BIERE - BIER - BIRRA DOPPIO MALTO - BEER
12% VOL. ALC.
1769
Bush
Beer 12%
Br. Dubuisson B 7904 Pipaix Belgique België
℮ 0,25L.
LOT
A|B|C|D|E|F|G|H|I|J|K|L|1|2|3|4|5|6|7

BIERE - BIER - BIRRA DOPPIO MALTO
12% VOL. ALC.
1769
Bush de Noël
Spéciale Noël
Br. Dubuisson 7904 Pipaix Belgique België
℮ 0,25L.
8.4 FL OZ
LOT.
A|B|C|D|E|F|G|H|I|J|K|L|1|2|3|4|5|6

Opposite *Oerbier means "original beer" and was the first one made by the Hartleer brothers. They brewed it in a wash tub at home before buying a small brewery.*

British pale ales in Belgium in the 1930s, a popularity which increased when British troops discovered the beer in World War Two. The beer is sold in the US under the name of Scaldis – Latin for Belgium's main river, the Schedlt – to avoid confusion with the Busch beer produced by international Anheuser-Busch, owners of Budweiser.

The amber-coloured beer is made from pale malt and caramalt with Styrian and Kent Goldings. The peppery, spicy Goldings dominate the palate along with delicious winey fruit and a hint of nuts from the darker malt. The beer has 42 units of bitterness. Primary fermentation lasts for a week in closed vessels and the beer is then cold conditioned for four to six weeks before being filtered but not pasteurised. A darker, dry-hopped version is produced for the Christmas season and called Bush de Noël, with an aroma like Dundee cake, sultana fruit in the mouth and a big vinous finish.

Brasserie Dubuisson Frères, Chaussée de Mons 28, 7904 Pipaix.

Mad Beer

De Dolle Arabier, Boskeun, Oerbier and Stille Nacht.

There cannot be a definitive style called mad beer but the De Dolle Brouwers – "the Mad Brewers" – do not fit comfortably into any

other category of Belgian ales. It is a micro brewery driven by eccentricity, passion and enthusiasm, located in a small town near Ostend. It is open to the public at weekends and the bar/reception area has an enormous open fire that is a welcome sight in winter.

The brewery dates from the 1840s and seemed certain to close in 1980 when the owner was taken ill. But three keen home-brewing brothers, who had started with a beer kit bought from Boots the Chemist on a trip to England, bought the site and started to brew beer at the weekends. The driving force is a

Opposite *The Mad Brewers make several seasonal ales. Arabier contains a joke about a parrot that even the Monty Python team would find hard to understand. Boskeun is Bunny Beer and is brewed for the Easter period.*

combination of one of the brothers, Kris Harteleer, and his mother, known as Mutti, who often leads the public tours of the brewery. The brewhouse is tiny, cramped and packed with antique equipment: a pre-World War One mash tun, a copper fired by direct flame, and an open wort cooler or "cool ship". Untreated water comes from six wells in the town.

The main brew is the 7 per cent abv Oerbier, "original brew", first made in a wash tub in the Harteleer's home. It uses six malts, including caramalt and black malt, with Belgian hops from Poperinge and East Kent Goldings. It has a sour plums aroma and is bitter-sweet in the mouth with a fruity finish.

The 8 per cent Arabier is a summer ale: the name comes from a Flemish joke incapable of translation, though a parrot is involved and appears on the label. It is a hazy bronze colour with a damson jam and spicy hops aroma, rich fruit and hops in the mouth and a big fruity finish. It is dry hopped with Goldings.

Boskeun – Easter Bunny, 8 per cent abv – is another seasonal ale and is sweetened with honey. Stille Nacht, an 8 per cent Christmas beer, has a massive marmalade fruit aroma and palate, a dry finish and a hint of lactic sourness. All the beers are bottle conditioned: Stille Nacht in particular will improve and deepen with laying down.

De Dolle Brouwers, Roeselarestraat 128, 8600 Diksmuide.

Bos
Keun
CAT.S 33 CL
SPECIAAL PAASBIER
BREWED & BOTTLED
BY DDB 8160
ESEN
BELGIUM
ALCVOL %7° HOGE GISTING MET NAGISTING IN DE FLES.
GEBROUWEN MET MOUT, HOP, GIST, RIETSUIKER EN MUD.
NIET GEFILTERD–NIET GEPASTEURISEERD–MET SMAAKEVOLUTIE.
GEBOTTELD DAT:1 2 3 4 5 6 7 8 9 10 11 12 94 95 96 97 98

33 CL℮ FL. OZ 11.6
CAT.S
ara bier
BREWED & BOTTLED BY
DE DOLLE BROUWERS IN
8160 ESEN BELGIUM
SPECIAAL ONGEFILTERD, NIET GEPASTEURISEERD BIER VAN HOGE GISTING
MET NAGISTING IN DE FLES. BELGISCHE DENSITEIT 7° ALC VOL % 8°
GEBROUWEN MET ENKEL WATER, MOUT, HOP, GIST, RUWE HOPPING EN DE BESTE
ZORGEN VAN DE DOLLE BROUWERS - BIER MET SMAAKEVOLUTIE.
KOEL SCHENKEN +10° GEBOTTELD 1 2 3 4 5 6 7 8 9 10 11 12 89 90 91 92

Czech Republic

The modern Czech Republic includes the major region of Bohemia which gave birth to one of the world's classic beer styles in the last century. While commercial lagering (or cold storing) of beer was developed in neighbouring Bavaria, the first pale gold lager beer came from Pilsen, the industrial powerhouse of Bohemia. Pilsen bequeathed a style called Pilsner, Pilsener or plain Pils – a style that has been bowdlerized beyond recognition in many countries. Too late, the brewers of the first golden beer added the word *urquell* to their brand, meaning "original source". Today, only the beers from Pilsen – Pilsner Urquell and Gambrinus – are allowed to use the term Pilsner, which is the equivalent of a French *appellation contrôlée.* The two other great lager styles are Prague beers, from the capital, and Budweisers from the South Bohemian town of Ceské Budejovice, formerly known as Budweis in German. Both the Pilsner and Budweiser styles have come under attack while Prague beers are brewed traditionally thanks to the determination of the British company Bass – which has a controlling interest in Prague Breweries – to remain true to proper lagering techniques.

At Pilsner Urquell traditional wooden fermenters and lagering tanks have been replaced by stainless steel, robbing the beer of some of its wonderful complexity. The brewers of Budweiser Budvar face a different problem:

Opposite
The Moorish-style water tower at the Pilsner Urquell Brewery in Pilsen, where the first golden lager in the world was produced in 1842 and transformed brewing throughout the world.

the world's biggest brewer, Anheuser-Busch of the United States, is using the courts to register its Budweiser brand, which would prevent the Czech beer from appearing in those countries where American "Bud" is registered first.

Brewing politics aside, the best way to enjoy Czech beers is to visit the country and enjoy them in unpasteurized draught form in bars and restaurants. You will also find examples of dark lagers that predate by several centuries the 19th-century pale beer revolution. (Note: the beers listed are what the Czechs call 12 degree beers, which are the versions exported. Most breweries also produce 10 degree beers for everyday drinking.)

BUDWEISER BUDVAR

Opposite
Old Budvar labels. Since the Budweiser Budvar Brewery opened early in the 20th century it has struggled to avoid litigation with the American brewer of Budweiser. When the Czech Budweiser was banned in the US, Budvar tried to sell it under the name Crystal.

The beers from the town known as Budweis in German are distinctively different to those from Pilsen. Budweiser Budvar is a wonderfully smooth yet complex beer, lagered for 90 days, one of the longest conditioning periods in the world. It is brewed from pale barley malt from neighbouring Moravia, Zatec hops (Saaz in German) and soft brewing liquor from a deep, natural underwater lake.

Mashing, lautering and boiling take place in superb copper vessels. Primary fermentation is in open square vessels, lagering is in closed conicals. The beer is 5 per cent abv and has around 21 units of bitterness. It has a rich and aromatic nose of malt, vanilla and perfumy

BUDVAR BREWERIES OF ČESKÉ BUDĚJOVICE N.C. MADE IN CZECHOSLOVAKIA
Budvar

BŘEZŇÁK
SPECIELNÍ 15°
ČESKÝ AKCIOVÝ PIVOVAR Č. BUDĚJOVICE
Budvar

FINEST CZECH
Budvar
LAGER BEER
BUDVAR, BREWERIES OF ČESKÉ BUDĚJOVICE N.C.,
MADE IN CZECHOSLOVAKIA

SPECIÁLNÍ
Budvar
15° Granát
JIHOČESKÉ PIVOVARY N.P. Č. BUDĚJOVICE

IMPORTED
ORIGINAL
BOHEMIAN
BudweiserBeer
FROM BUDWEIS CITY
BOHEMIAN BREWERY LTD.
ČESKÉ BUDĚJOVICE
BUDWEIS
CZECHOSLOVAKIA
CONTAINS 11 FLUID OUNCES NET
IMPORTED BY
PAUL OSTRUK
120 W. 42.ND ST. NEW YORK CITY
PERMIT AB I No 1770

BUDVAR BREWERIES OF ČESKÉ BUDĚJOVICE N.C. MADE IN CZECHOSLOVAKIA
Budvar

hops, there is rich malt in the mouth with a long finish that is a brilliant balance of malt, hops and a final hint of delicious apple fruit from the house yeast.

The brewery was opened in 1895, some 25 years after the Anheuser-Busch brewery in the United States launched its Budweiser beer.

Ironically, it is the other brewery in the town of Ceské Budejovice, Samson, which brewed a beer called Budweiser before Anheuser-Busch, but dropped the brand name early this century. (Budweiser Budvar is not available in the United States.)

Budejovicky Budvar, Karoliny Svetlé 4, 370 21 Ceské Budejovice.

Pilsner Urquell

The entrance gate is shaped like a triumphal Napoleonic arch as befits one of the world's great and historic breweries. In the 1830s the citizens of Pilsen were dissatisfied with the quality of the local beers. Matters came to a head when an entire batch of stale beer had to be poured down the drain. Innkeepers banded together to form a new "citizen's brewery" and they hired a young but experienced Bavarian brewer named Josef Grolle who was skilled in the new techniques of cold fermentation and lagering. In 1842 Grolle produced a pale gold beer that took Pilsen and then the world by storm: at the time the lagers of Bavaria were still brown in colour as malt was cured over wood fires. But Grolle's employers installed a

Above
The magnificent Napoleonic entrance to the Pilsner Urquell brewery.
Opposite
A Budvar delivery truck before the Second World War. The beer was labelled "Budbrau" for German-speaking areas.

British coke-fired kiln that produced pale malt. The resultant beer was a revelation and brewers worldwide rushed to emulate him. Until the 1990s, Pilsner Urquell was fermented and lagered in wooden vessels that gave the complex beer some of its oak and tannin character. But the wooden vessels are now confined to a museum and fermentation and lagering are carried out in stainless steel vessels. As a result, the beer is more fully "attenuated", which means more malt sugars turn to alcohol. This leads to a drier beer with a more pronounced hop character.

It is 4.5 per cent abv and has a resounding 40 units of bitterness.The raw materials are Pilsner malt and Zatec hops – the hops are added three times during the boil. The beer is lagered for 70 days. It has an enormous bouquet of aromatic hops, soft malt and honey, with malt, vanilla and hops in the mouth and a long, complex finish that is a beautiful balance of tart hops and rich malt.

Plzensky Pradroj,
U Prazdroje 304 97, Plzen.

STAROPRAMEN BLONDE & DARK

Staropramen means "old spring" and it was the naturally soft waters of Prague that enabled the brewery, founded in 1869, to produce its smooth and tartly bitter beers in the industrial Smichov district of the Czech capital. The beer was praised by Franz Josef I, the Austro-Hungarian emperor from 1848, and his accolade boosted sales of the beer.

In 1992 Staropramen and two other Prague-based breweries, Branik and Méstan, merged following the end of state control, and welcomed a substantial investment from the British brewing group, Bass, which has vigorously exported the beer. While many other Czech breweries are transferring to modern brewing methods, Bass has insisted that Staropramen should maintain its support for horizontal lagering tanks, rather than upright conicals. This may seem an arcane point but the different method is important: secondary fermentation in horizontal tanks is slower than in conicals and not all the malt sugars turn to alcohol. As a result, the finished beer has a rounder character, avoiding a lack of balance in which hops dominate the malt. Staropramen Blonde lager is 5 per cent abv,

Opposite
The original Pilsner.
Above
Staropramen is the leading Prague brewery.

with a rich malty aroma balanced by perfumy hops, a firm malty palate and a lingering finish with a good balance of malt and hops and creamy vanilla hints. Staropramen Dark (4.5 per cent) is a fine example of the dark lagers that predate the golden variety. It has a deep ruby-chestnut colour, a fine fluffy head, a herbal and toffee-like aroma, a silky smooth palate and a rich finish with a delicate hops and dark malt character.

Prazské Pivovary [Prague Breweries], Nadrazni 84, 150 54 Prague 5-Smichov.

Black Regent

Opposite
Regent in Trebon has maintained the style of garnet-coloured dark lagers that predate the Pilsen revolution.

Not all Bohemian breweries turned their backs on dark beers following the Pilsner revolution of the mid-19th century. The Regent Brewery in Trebon, famous for its carp-filled lakes, makes a good pale lager, Bohemia Regent, broadly in the Budweiser style, but it is best known for its dark beer, which would once have been top fermented but is now a lager.

Regent has one of the finest brewhouses in the country: it had fallen into a poor state during the years of communist rule but since privatisation it has been busily refurbished. The brewery was founded in 1379 and was later moved by the noble Schwarzenberg family into their castle's armoury, where it was rebuilt with its own maltings. The brewing process is meticulous: mashing and boiling take 12 hours, followed by primary fermentation for 12 days and lagering for 90 days. Black Regent (4.5 per cent abv) is brewed from pale, caramalt and dark malts, is ruby-red in colour, with an appealing aroma of hops and bitter chocolate, dark malt in the mouth, and a hoppy/malty finish reminiscent of cappuccino coffee.

Pivovar Regent, Trocnovské
nám. 379 14 Trebon.

France

France has a beer tradition, though it has to be teased out. Wine is the all-dominating drink and its seeming omnipotence tends to mask the fact that beer was once brewed throughout the country. The ancient Gauls were great brewers of *cervoise*, from the Latin for ale, and at the turn of the 20th century there were still 3,000 French breweries. Today there are around 40 and, with the exception of a Heineken plant in Marseilles, they are all concentrated in the north. The decline is linked to the fact that beer never enjoyed the hauteur of wine, even though both are drunk in cafés called brasseries, which means breweries. Beer was seen as a simple refresher and few therefore objected to the industrialization of the product, which led to the rise of a handful of brewing giants. Today the food group BSN with its brewing subsidiary Kronenbourg controls around 50 per cent of the beer market. Heineken, which includes Pelforth of Lille, accounts for a further 25 per cent and the Belgian Interbrew group has another large slice with its lagers Jupiler and Stella Artois. The Strasbourg area, with its historic German connection, produces the bulk of French beer, mainly unremarkable blonde lagers. To discover the true heart of French brewing you have to start in Lille and find the roots of the beer style in the Nord-Pas de Calais region that is known as *bières de garde* – "beers to keep". The style has rural origins and has

Opposite
A selection of the perennial favourites and seasonal specialities available from the Brasserie de St-Sylvestre deep in the heart of hop-growing country in French Flanders.

bière des flandr
BRASSEE EN FLANDRES
Bock du Moulin
de St SYLVESTRE 59114 - BIERE BOCK 33cl
BIÈRE
EN FLANDRE
Bière de Noël
3 MONTS · 3 MONTS · 3 MONTS
BRASSÉE EN FLANDRE
DE SAINT SYLVESTRE
BRASSERIE DE SAINT SYLVESTRE
3 MONTS
BIÈRE DE FLANDRE
CAT. S. e 75cl
FERMENTATION HAUTE
BIÈRE DE MARS
LABEL REGIONAL
NORD-PAS DE CALAIS
Homologation n°04-85 — Décret 17.06.83
BIERES SPECIALES DU NORD
Arrêté Préfectoral 15.11.85
Bière certifiée et contrôlée par l'Association
QUALITE
nord - pas de calais
Ophélia
24,5cl

Opposite
Pastor Ale is brewed by the Lepers family in a converted farm, pointing to the powerful rural roots of the style known as bière de garde.

obvious connections with the saisons of French-speaking Wallonia across the Belgian border. These keeping beers were once brewed exclusively on farms: farmers took the produce of the fields – barley, wheat and hops – and made strong, often dark, top-fermenting beers in the spring that were drunk by their families and workers during the hot summer months when brewing was not possible. An ancient hop-growing area stretches from Ypres in Belgium down into French Flanders while the Champagne and Burgundy areas, by an ironic twist, produce fine malting barley. The interest in *bière de garde* has led to a small revival: there are now a few dozen producers of the style, energetically defended by the consumer group Les Amis de la Bière. Some, but not all, the artisanal brewers of the region are experimenting with bottom-working lager yeasts rather than top-fermenting cultures in order to give greater stability to the beers in bottle. It would be a shame if the true character of the style was weakened in order to appease the supermarket god known as Shelf Life.

Annoeullin Pastor Ale and L'Angelus

Bertrand and Yvonne Lepers bring a touch of humour to their *bière de garde*, Pastor Ale. The punning name is emphasised by the sub-title *c'est une symphonie*. Worse things are done to Beethoven today than to enshrine him on a

beer label. The tiny brewery, in a small town between Lille and Lens, is based in buildings that were once part of a farm: the beer ferments in horizontal tanks in cellars that used to be cattle byres. And in the French-Flanders tradition, the ancient mash tun doubles as a copper after the wort has been clarified. Pastor Ale is 6.5 per cent abv and is brewed from pale malt only. Local hops are used for bitterness, with Saaz for aroma. Primary fermentation lasts

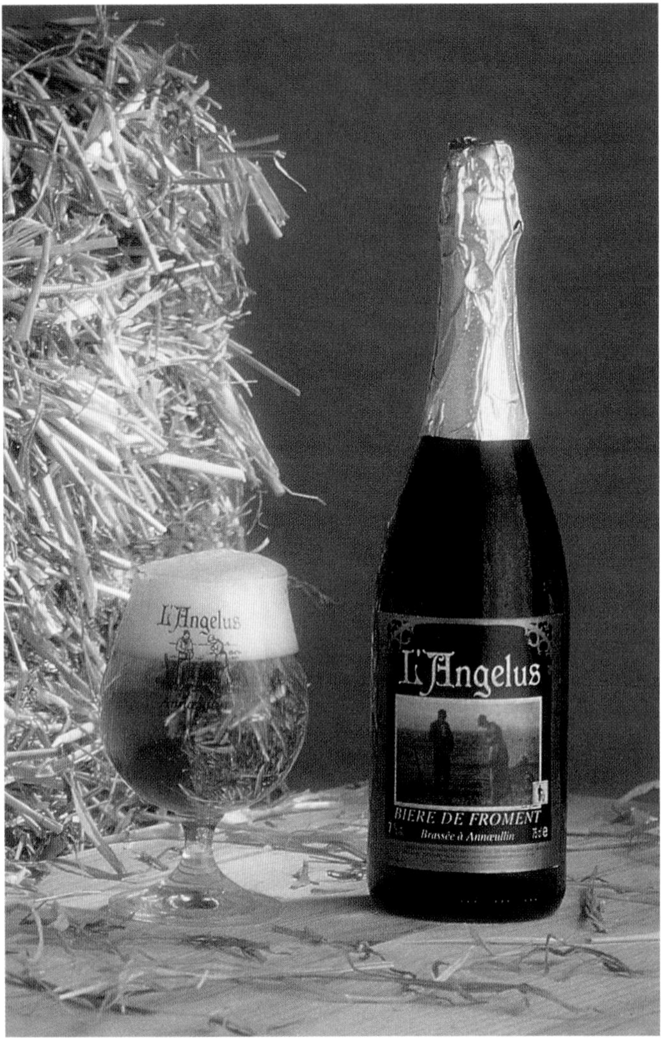
L'Angelus
L'Angelus
BIERE DE FROMENT
Brassée à Annœullin

for a week, followed by two weeks for conditioning. As with the other beers from the brewery, the house yeast imparts a powerful orange-citric fruitiness to the aroma and palate, balanced by earthy and spicy hops. The other main product is a wheat beer called L'Angelus – Bière de Froment ("wheat beer"), 7.3 per cent. Buck wheat in flour form accounts for 30 per cent of the grist. It is bronze-coloured and has a powerful tangerine aroma backed by spicy hops with more tart fruit in the mouth and a long, bitter-sweet finish.
Brasserie Lepers, 4 Place du Général de Gaulle, 59112 Annoeullin.

Opposite
Angelus from the Lepers' brewery is a wheat beer with a powerful aroma and flavour of tangerine fruit.
Below
Ch'ti means "it suits you" in the Picardian dialect.

CH'TI BRUNE AND BLONDE

In the tradition of the region, Castelain started life as a farm-brewery but its beers were produced as much for miners as for farm labourers. The area just north of Lens was the heart of the French coalfields but all the pits have closed and the only reminder is the grey and ghostly figure of a helmeted miner on the bottle labels of Ch'ti, a Picardian dialect word based on *c'est toi* – "it suits you". The farm and brewery date from 1926 and was bought by the Castelain family in 1966. Yves Castelain, the young and energetic current owner, brews in gleaming copper vessels visible from the street, and produces around 28,000 hectolitres a year. He uses Flemish and French barleys, with local hops and some German Tettnanger or

Opposite
Jenlain is the best-known of the bière de garde *style.*
Above
The Castelain Brewery in the heart of the former mining region in northern France.

Hallertauer varieties. He is a convinced convert to lager yeast but his beers, fermented at 15° C /60°F, have a pronounced fruity character. Primary fermentation lasts for 10 to 12 days, followed by up to two months for maturing.

Ch'ti Blonde is made from four malts, the Brune from eight, including Munich, cara-Munich and torrefied varieties. Both are 6.5 per cent abv. The Blonde has a rich and enticing aroma and palate of biscuity malt and tart hops, with a firm malty palate and some citric fruit, and a long finish dominated by hops and tart fruit. The Brune has a strong hint of raisins in the mouth and some vinous, port-wine notes in the finish. The brewery also produces a 4.6 organic Jade, with more hop character, pungent and perfumy, with sweet malt in the mouth and a fruity finish, Saint Arnoldus (7.5 per cent),

rich and fruity, bottled on its yeast and named after the patron saint of brewers, and Korma (5.9 per cent), made from seven malts, with a chaff-like aroma, big vinous palate and a bitter-sweet finish.
Brasserie Castelain, 13 rue de Pasteur, Bénifontaine, 62410 Wingles.

JENLAIN

This is the beer that brought the style of *bière de garde* to a wider audience than northern France. In its handsome corked and cradled bottle, it proved that beer could have the elegance and finesse of fine wine. It became a cult drink with students in Lille in the 1980s and featured prominently in festivals and celebrations in the city.

As the name Duyck stresses, the family is of Flemish stock and they had been brewing long before Félix Duyck started production on a farm in the village of Jenlain south-east of Valenciennes in 1922. The business is now run by his son Robert and grandson Raymond. Production has grown to 90,000 hectolitres a year but brewing remains in traditional vessels, most of them bought second-hand.

Malts from Flanders, Champagne and Burgundy are used, along with four hop varieties from Belgium, France, Germany and Slovenia.

Above
A copper brewing vessel at Jenlain.
Opposite
Labels old and new for St Sylvestre's 3 Monts.

Jenlain (6.5 per cent abv) is russet-coloured, spicy and malty, with hints of smoky malt, vanilla and citric fruit.

The beer was top-fermented for years until the Duycks experimented with a lager culture but recent reports suggest they have returned to the true ale method of production.

Duyck also brews a paler Printemps ("spring") beer and a seasonal Christmas beer.
Brasserie Duyck, 113 route Nationale, 59144 Jenlain.

TROIS MONTS

The Flemish word *cappel* in the address tells you that this farmhouse brewery is deep in French Flanders, in hop-growing country between Steenvoorde and Hazebrouck. It dates from the 1850s, though it may date back to the 16th century. It has been run since the 1920s by the Ricour family; now by Pierre Ricour, his wife and sons. The copper is coal-fired and he uses English and French malts with local Brewers' Gold and German Tettnanger hops, and top-fermenting yeast cultures. Trois Monts, a classic *bière de garde*, is named after three local hills: even such small bumps are worthy of celebration in the flatlands of Flanders. The golden beer is 8.5 per cent abv and is brewed with Pilsner malt and some brewing sugar. It has a pronounced winey and fruity aroma and palate, with strong hints of yeast and alcohol and some lactic sourness. An abbey-style *Bière de Templiers* of the same strength, creamy and fruity and bottled on its yeast, and a Christmas ale are also made. There is also a *Bière de Mars*: St Sylvestre pioneered the rebirth of strong, pale March beers which have been taken up by other small brewers and even the giants. Despite the name, the beer is brewed in December and stored until March and then drunk to celebrate spring.

Brasserie de St-Sylvestre, 1 rue de la Chappelle, 59114 St-Sylvestre-Cappel.

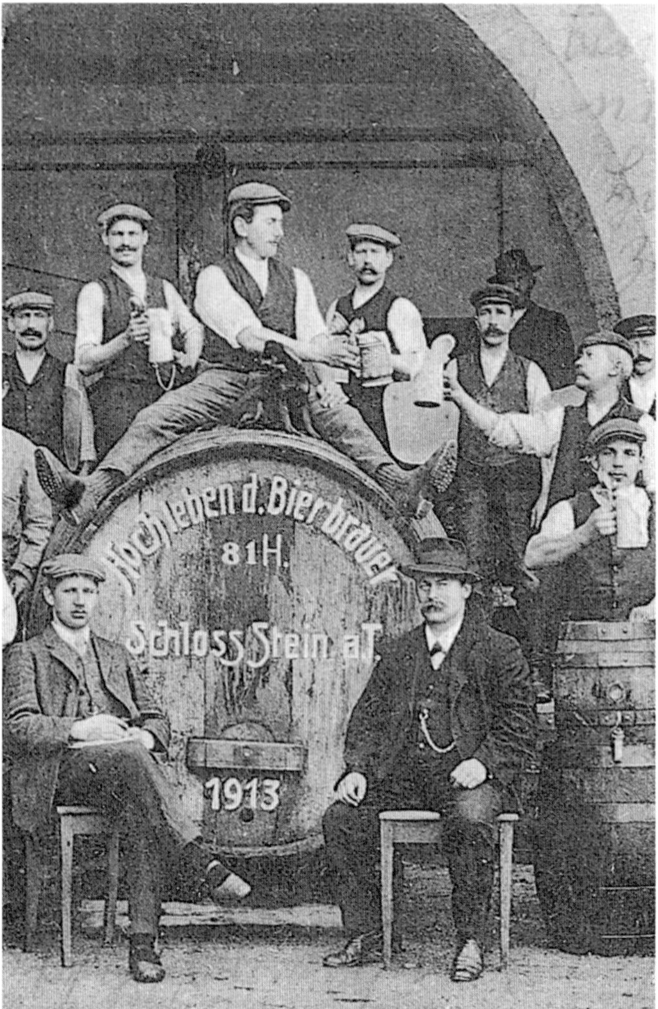
Hochleben d. Bierbrauer
81 H.
Schloss Stein a.T.
1913

GERMANY

Germany is the world's greatest beer-drinking country. The Czechs – shorn of the wine-loving Slovaks – may just pip the Germans in the consumption per head league but with their verve and enthusiasm for beer, their downing of foaming steins, their use of beer to fuel every celebration and dodge the rigours of Lent, and in the surprising diversity of their styles, the Germans are unbeatable.

They have 1,300 breweries, an astonishing number at a time when in every other country save for the United States producers are falling as a result of closures and mergers. For the Germans, their small local breweries, often in villages and towns as well as the major cities, are part of their tradition, their culture and their birthright. And beer is underpinned by the *Reinheitsgebot*, the 16th-century "Pure Beer Pledge" that permits only malted barley and wheat, hops, water and yeast to be used, forbidding brewing sugars and cereal adjuncts. Although the European Court outlawed the *Reinheitsgebot* in the 1980s as a "restraint of trade", brewers and drinkers remain loyal to it. They are scornful of other countries' "chemi-beers" and imports have made little impact.

Germany is about more than just lager beer. Wheat, Alt and Kölsch beers pre-date the lager revolution of the 19th century and are members of the ale family. Wheat beers in particular are growing in popularity. And

Opposite
Bavarian brewery workers at Schloss Stein celebrate another year's successful brewing astride a giant lager cask in 1913.

German lager beers offer a rich diversity, from the uncompromisingly bitter and hoppy versions of the north to the rounded and malt-accented style in Munich. Dark lagers, which predate the Pilsner revolution, survive in abundance as do smoked beers. There are some splendidly strong and robust Bock beers, strong lagers first brewed by monks as their "liquid bread" to sustain them during the Lenten period, while spring, the Oktoberfest and Christmas all have their celebratory tipples.

ALTBIER
DIEBELS ALT

Alt means "old" and in the Düsseldorf region it refers to a type of beer that predates lagering and has an affinity with the brown ales of Belgium and the English Midlands. These top-fermenting ales were brewed to refresh industrial workers after long, sweaty shifts down mine shafts or in foundries.

Heavy industry, especially coal mining, has declined steeply in Düsseldorf but Alt not only retains its hold on working-class drinkers but has found a new audience among the younger generation. Alt is best enjoyed in the taverns of the cobbled Old Town, where the beer is brewed on the premises and served from wooden casks on the bar tops. The taste can be enjoyed in bottle thanks to Diebels, which manages to be both a family-owned brewery in the hamlet of Issum and also one of Germany's biggest brewers, producing approximately 1.7 million hectolitres a year.

Opposite
An artist's impression of the Diebels Brewery in Issum soon after it was built.
Above
Diebels Alt is the main brand of the Düsseldorf area.

Diebels Alt has a gravity of 1045 degrees and reaches 4.8 per cent abv, which means it is well attenuated, with most of the sugars turned to alcohol. It has a burnished copper colour and is made from 98 per cent Pilsner malt with two per cent roasted barley – more of a Scottish or Irish practice than a German one; other Alt brewers prefer to get their colour and "body" from Vienna or black malt. Hops are Northern Brewer for bitterness and Perle for aroma: they

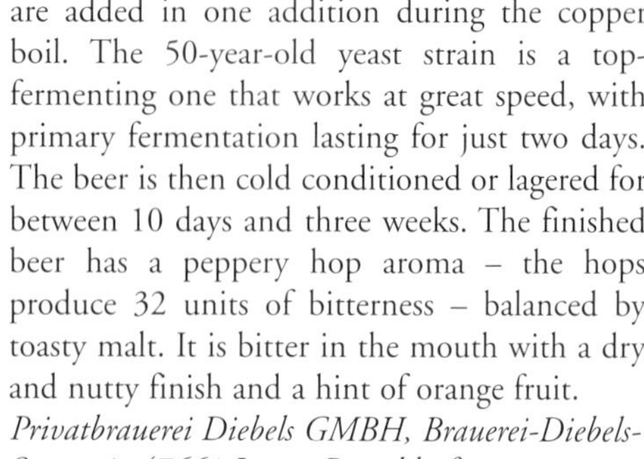

are added in one addition during the copper boil. The 50-year-old yeast strain is a top-fermenting one that works at great speed, with primary fermentation lasting for just two days. The beer is then cold conditioned or lagered for between 10 days and three weeks. The finished beer has a peppery hop aroma – the hops produce 32 units of bitterness – balanced by toasty malt. It is bitter in the mouth with a dry and nutty finish and a hint of orange fruit.
Privatbrauerei Diebels GMBH, Brauerei-Diebels-Strasse 1, 47661 Issum, Düsseldorf.

KÖLSCH

FRÜH KÖLSCH

No one outside Cologne (Köln in German) can call a beer *Kölsch*. The golden, top-fermenting beer is protected by a government ordinance similar to a French *appellation contrôlée* for wine. In 1985 all the Cologne brewers and the federal government signed a convention written on parchment with the seals of all the producers.

The reason why ale-style beers survive in both Cologne and neighbouring Düsseldorf is a result of temperament, a cool climate that does not call for chilled beers and the proximity of the Low Countries and their top-fermenting beers.

The classic Kölsch producer is P J Früh's court brewhouse in the city centre. The beer is 5 per cent abv, is made from pale malt only (some brewers use a small proportion of wheat) and is hopped with both Hallertauer and Tettnanger

Opposite
Früh is one of the specialist brewers of Kölsch, the golden ale protected by a city ordinance.
Left
An early photograph of waiters at P J Früh's brewhouse in Cologne.

varieties. After primary fermentation, the beer is conditioned for up to six weeks.

The yeast strain used – *obergäriges* or top-fermenting – is very greedy and turns most of the malt sugars to alcohol, producing a dry beer. It has delicate fruit on the aroma, is firmly malty in the mouth and has a dry finish with hops and tart fruit.

P J Früh Cölner Hofbräu, 12-14 Am Hof, 5000 Cologne.

WHEAT BEER

MAISEL'S HEFE-WEISSE

The Maisel Brothers' brewery produces one of Bavaria's classic wheat beers. It is 5.2 per cent abv, has a ruddy colour, an enticing aroma and palate of apples, and a dry, quenching, slightly sour finish. The label says it is both *weisse* and *weizen*: the terms, meaning "white" and "wheat", are interchangeable. *Hefe* means yeast, indicating that the beer is unfiltered, bottle-conditioned and cloudy when poured. In common with all wheat beers, it is a blend of both malted barley and malted wheat: barley malt has a higher level of natural enzymes that turn starches to sugar. Hallertauer hops are used sparingly as a preservative as too much bitterness would overpower the fruitiness that is typical of the style.

Maisel is the biggest of the city's breweries. Although the present plant was installed in the 1970s, the original brewing equipment, including 1930s steam engines, can be seen in the brewery's museum – listed in the *Guinness Book of Records* as the world's biggest brewery museum. Maisel also brews a good Pilsner, a Dunkel dark lager and an intensely fruity top-fermenting *Dampfbier* – "steam beer" – at 5 per cent. True to brewery tradition, Maisel is run by two brothers, Hans and Oscar, descendants of Hans and Eberhardt Maisel, who founded the brewery in 1887.

Gerbrüder Maisel's Brauerei, Hindenburgstrasse 9, 95445 Bayreuth.

Opposite
The impressive Maisel Brewery in Bayreuth, producer of a classic wheat beer.

Below
Schneider of Kelheim was the first commercial brewer of wheat licensed by the Bavarian royal family.

SCHNEIDER WEISSE AND AVENTINUS

Schneider, based in the heart of the Hallertau hop region of Bavaria, is the classic brewer of wheat beer. In 1850 Georg Schneider was granted a licence by the Bavarian royal family to brew wheat beer in their Munich *Hofbräuhaus* – "royal court brewhouse". Until then wheat beer had been brewed and drunk only by the aristocracy. In spite of the spread of lager brewing, Schneider's wheat beer was a revelation. He moved to a new site in Munich and opened a second brewery in Kelheim:

Right
A powerful dopplebock, a spicy and chocolatey beer that makes a good late-night drink.

production is now concentrated there following the destruction of his Munich plant in World War Two. The Kelheim brewery makes around 300,000 hectolitres a year, 90 per cent of which is the 5.4 per cent abv Weisse. Bavarian barley and wheat malts are blended in the ratio of 60 to 40, with some Vienna and dark malts added for flavour, body and to give the finished beer its attractive copper colour. Hersbrücker hops from the Hallertau give the beer 14 to 15 units of bitterness. Primary fermentation takes places in open vessels – a rare sight in Germany. The beer is bottled with a dose of yeast and some sugar-rich wort and is then warm conditioned for a week to encourage a second fermentation. The beer is then held in cold store for a fortnight before being released.

It has a complex bouquet of banana, cloves and nutmeg, there is tart fruit in the mouth and a creamy, fruity finish with hints of bubblegum – bubblegum is a common flavour in wheat beers and comes from the special top-fermenting strain of yeast. The 8 per cent Aventinus is a *doppelbock* – a doubly strong bock beer with caramalt, a type of crystal malt made in Bamberg. It is a deep tawny colour with a spicy aroma and hints of chocolate, vinous fruit in the mouth and chocolate and cloves in the finish. It is the perfect nightcap.

G Schneider & Sohn, 1-5 Emil Ott Strasse, 8420 Kelheim.

Below
Berliner Kindl is one of just two breweries that produce a style once called the "Champagne of the North".

BERLIN WHEAT BEER
BERLINER KINDL

When Napoleon's troops reached Berlin they dubbed the local wheat beers the "Champagne of the North". The origins of the style are unknown but it is possible that migrating Huguenots learnt to brew the beer as they travelled north from France through Flanders.

Berliner Weisse, like a Brussels lambic, is deliberately soured during production. A specific lactic culture was isolated early this century by Professor Max Delbrück at Berlin University's brewing school: the culture is now named *lacto-bacillus delbrücki* in his honour. The beer, just 2.5 per cent abv, is brewed from soft water, 70 per cent barley malt and 30 per cent wheat malt. Northern Brewer hops

Opposite
Berliner Kindl in all its pomp in the 19th century. After the Second World War, the brewery was faithfully rebuilt in the Bauhaus style.

produce just 10 units of bitterness. After mashing and boiling, the lactic culture is added first to start acidification, followed by a top-fermenting culture. Fermentation lasts for a week followed by several days of cold conditioning. The beer is then filtered, bottled with a dose of yeast and *kräusened* with partially fermented wort. Drunk naturally, the beer is tart, mouth-puckering, and acidic rather

Opposite
The fairy-tale setting of Kaltenberg Castle south of Munich.

like freshly-squeezed lemons. It is wonderfully refreshing but in Berlin drinkers add a dose of syrup, such as woodruff or raspberry, to cut the acidity.

Berliner Weisse is now produced by only two brewers and the style is in serious decline. It needs and deserves support.

Berliner Kindl Brauerei, 50 Werbellin Strasse, Neu Köln, 1000 Berlin.

DARK LAGER

KALTENBERG KÖNIG LUDWIG DUNKEL

The castle brewery south of Munich is owned by Crown Prince Luitpold, a member of the Bavarian royal family. When he took over the family estate in 1976 he decided to turn brewing from a sideline into a commercial enterprise on the sensible grounds that he was unlikely to ascend to the redundant German throne. He brews wheat beer and Pilsner but he has turned the Dunkel dark lager into a classic and it is now his main brand.

The 5.6 per cent abv beer is well attenuated, with most of the brewing sugars turned to alcohol. It is brewed from pale and a Belgian dark malt and is hopped with Hersbrücker and Tettnanger varieties, which produce 24 to 26 units of bitterness. Prince Luitpold – who names the beer after one of his royal ancestors, King Ludwig – also adds hops to the finished beer in the British style known as "dry

hopping". The beer is *kräusened* during the lagering period, which means that some partially fermented wort is added to encourage a second fermentation. Lagering takes place in pitch-lined wooden vessels in the castle cellars. The beer has a pronounced bitter-hoppy character from aroma to finish, balanced by dark malt, coffee and bitter fruit.
Schlossbrauerei Kaltenberg, Augsburger Strasse 41, 82256 Fürstenfeldbruck.

KÖSTRITZER SCHWARZBIER

When the wall between the two Germanys fell, a beer style that had been lost from sight for 40 years came out from under the rubble. Dr Axel Simon, chairman of the Bitburger Brewery in the Rhineland, hurried east to buy up a plant producing beer he remembered his mother drinking when he was a breast-feeding baby.

In common with English milk stouts, the black beer – *schwarzbier* – of the Thuringian region was regarded as a tonic. When the poet Goethe was once ill, a friend noted, "He is not eating but luckily we have some Köstritzer beer". Older drinkers liked to beat sugar and egg into the beer and the brewery produced a sweetened version. Now that the *Reinheitsgebot* again covers the old eastern sector, the sweetened version has been phased out and the strength has been increased from 3.5 per cent to 4.6 per cent abv. The Köstritzer beer differs from the dark lagers of Bavaria: it uses some

roasted malt and is darker and more opaque. At one time it was exported to Britain as "porter" though the beer is bottom fermented.

It is brewed from local pale malt, darker Munich malt and some roasted malt. Hüller hops for bitterness and Hallertau Mittelfrüh for aroma create 35 units of bitterness. Local spring water is softened. It has an aroma of dark fruit, malt loaf and bitter chocolate, with a creamy palate and a long, complex finish with bitter roasted malt, coffee and chocolate, and a good underpinning of hops.

Köstritzer Schwarzbierbrauerei, Heinrich Schütz Strasse, Bad Köstritz 6514, Thüringen.

Opposite
The black beer from Bad Köstritz was rediscovered when the wall between East and West Germany came down.
Above
A 1930s painting showing a Köstritzer brewery worker enjoying a stein after a hard day's labour.

PALE LAGERS

BITBURGER PREMIUM PILS

The small town of Bitburg in the Eifel region of the Rhineland is a long way from Pilsen but the story of Theobald Simon's brewery shows the impact that Pilsner beer had on the rest of Europe. It began as a farmhouse brewery in 1817 making top-fermenting dark beers but by 1884 it was producing Pilsner, using ice from surrounding lakes to store the beer. The company also adhered to a German court ruling that brewers must add the suffix "-er" to the labels of their Pils to avoid any suggestion

they came from Pilsen. The fortunes of Bitburger were boosted when a railway line was built linking the town with the steelworks of the Saar. Brewing today is divided between the superb old copper brewhouse in the town and a state-of-the-art new plant on a greenfield site in the suburbs. The malt and hop grists are complex: Alexis, Arena and Steiner barleys, Hersbrücker, Hülle, Perle and Tettnanger hops. The beer has three hop additions in the kettle, is 4.6 per cent with 37 to 38 units of bitterness. It is lagered for three months and is not pasteurized. It is an exceptionally dry beer, with a rich malt aroma underscored by

floral hops, soft malt in the mouth, and a long finish dominated by hop bitterness and some citric fruit.
Bitburger Privatbrauerei Th. Simon, Postfach 189, 5520 Bitburg-Eifel.

DAB EXPORT

Dortmund is the great steel and coal mining city of the Ruhr. It has had a brewing tradition since the 13th century and was famous for its wheat beers until bottom fermentation was embraced in the 19th. With it came a malty, rounded, full-bodied beer that was sold widely throughout Germany and across the border into the Netherlands, activity that gave the style the name of Export.

Dortmunder Actien was founded by the Fischer family in 1868 and went public in 1872: Actien indicates a company that has publicly-quoted shares. The decline of heavy industry has led to DAB and its rivals down-playing the importance of their Exports and concentrating on drier Pils: the original style needs to be savoured and saved. Export is 5 per cent abv and blends some Munich malt with Pilsner malt to give the beer a burnished bronze colour. Bavarian hop varieties produce between 20 to 25 units of bitterness. Fermentation is stopped to leave some malt sugars in the brew: in the manner of all beers brewed in heavy industrial areas,

Opposite
Pre-Second World War trucks loaded with wooden casks of Bitburger beer. The brewery's Pils found a vast audience when Bitburg was linked by rail to the steelworks of the Saar.

sweetness is needed to restore drinkers' lost energy. The beer has a rich malt aroma, a firm malty body and a bitter-sweet finish with a late burst of hops. The style is much admired and copied in the Netherlands, where it is called "Dort" for short.

Dortmunder Actien Brauerei, 20 Steiger Strasse, 4600 Dortmund 1.

PINKUS MÜLLER SPEZIAL

Pinkus Müller, in the quaint old university city of Münster, is a highly individualistic brewer, using organic malt and hops. This is a small brewery, producing around 10,000 hectolitres a year, yet it is renowned in Germany and in export markets for its devotion to ingredients that are free from chemical sprays.

It has been on its present site since 1816, when it began life as a *chocalatier* and bakery as well as a brewery. The sixth generation of the family runs the company.

Brewing takes place next to a tavern specialising in local cuisine: one of its sweet specialities is a syrup made from strawberries, peaches or oranges which are added to the house Altbier to cut down its acidity. (The Alt is an intriguing oddity, for the malts are a blend of barley and

wheat and is therefore not brewed in the Düsseldorf style.) Spezial (5.2 per cent abv) is a stunning premium lager beer. It is brewed from organic Bioland Gerstenbräu Pilsner malt and organic hops from the Hallertau, where a few growers have set aside fields where the plants are not sprayed with herbicides and pesticides. Spezial is lagered for a full three months and emerges with a rounded malt aroma and palate and a dry finish in which the hops dominate.

As well as the Alt (5.1 per cent) Pinkus Müller brews a 5.2 per cent Hefe Weizen and a dry, aromatic Pils.

Brauerei Pinkus Müller, 4-10 Kreuz Strasse, 4400 Münster, Nordrhein-Westfalen.

Opposite
Pinkus Müller beers from Münster use only organic ingredients.

Above
A drinking session got out of hand at Pinkus Müller's brewery, and the owner of a local zoo painted a donkey to look like a zebra and tied a servant to its back.

SPATEN PILSENER AND MÄRZEN

Opposite
Spaten Pils is a classic of the Munich style of brewing, developed by Gabriel Sedlmayr, a member of the brewery's ruling family.
Above
Old labels for Spaten beer.

Spaten is where the lager revolution began. This is where Gabriel Sedlmayr the Younger, a member of the family that owns Spaten, took the centuries-old practice of storing beer at low temperatures in ice-filled caves, and turned it into a mass-market drink with the aid of the new technologies of the industrial revolution: ice-making machines, steam power and yeast cultivation. Sedlmayr's first lager beers were dark. They appeared in the 1830s and the first pale lager did not go on sale until the 1890s. The Munich style of Pilsner, as exemplified at Spaten, is closer to the Pilsen version than the more austere, flinty versions brewed in the north of Germany. Spaten Pils, 5.2 per cent abv, is a bronze-gold colour from the slightly darker malt favoured in Munich, has a rich,

slightly toasty aroma with delicate perfumy hops, a full, bitter-sweet palate and a long, lingering finish that is a superb balance of malt and Bavarian hops. Ur-Märzen is the classic Oktoberfest beer, brewed in March and stored until the festival opens in the autumn. The "Ur" in the title is short for *Urtyp* or Original. Sedlmayr worked in close conjunction with the renowned Austrian brewer Anton Dreher who also had a pivotal role to play in lager techniques and pioneered the use of an amber malt cured to a higher temperature than pale

varieties. Spaten's Märzen is 5.6 per cent abv, has a burnished red-gold colour, and a big malt-accented aroma and palate – but the maltiness is clean, quenching and spicy, not cloying. There is a good balance of hops in the long bitter-sweet finish: the beer has 25 units of bitterness. The brewery's odd name comes from *Spaten* meaning "malt shovel" and *Franziskaner* meaning "Franciscan": a member of the Sedlmayr family once owned an old Munich brewery built next to a Franciscan monastery.
Spaten-Franziskaner-Bräu, Mars Strasse, 8000 Munich.

BOCK

EINBECKER UR-BOCK

Bavarians will tell you that *Bock* is a style unique to their region but its origins are in Saxony in the town of Einbeck, a major brewing centre since at least the 14th century which exported its beers vigorously as a member of the Hanseatic League.

Today Einbeck road signs proclaim it to be "Beer City" and the labels of Einbecker beer carry the slogan *Ohne Einbeck gäb's kein Bockbier* – "Without Einbeck there would be no Bock beer". The beer style was given considerable credibility when Martin Luther, leader of the Protestant Reformation, drank it to sustain him during the Diet of Worms in 1521 when he was excommunicated from the church for heresy. The term *Bock* stems from

the abbreviation of *Einbeck* to *Beck*, which became *Bock* in the Bavarian dialect. The first Bocks would have been dark and top-fermented but are now members of the lager family. Einbecker brews three Bocks, all of which are labelled "Ur-Bock – Original Bock" and all with strengths of 6.9 per cent abv. Soft water from deep wells, Brunswick malt, and Northern Brewer, Perle and Hersbrücker hops are used. The beers have a rich, rounded maltiness that avoids being cloying as a result of a long lagering that lasts from between six to 10 weeks. The pale Hell, with 38 units of bitterness, has an appealing malt aroma and palate with a late burst of hops in the finish. The Dunkel has the same level of bitterness with aroma and palate dominated by rich malt with hints of dark fruit and coffee, and again

Opposite
Ur-Bock means "original Bock" and is Einbeck's method of stamping its authenticity on the beer.

Above
An image of Martin Luther was used on early Einbeck labels. He drank the beer during his trial and excommunication for heresy.

Opposite
Drawing a crowd...an old poster portraying the pulling power of Paulaner's Munich beers.

the hops make a late entrance in the dry malt, hops and fruit finish. A Maibock, on sale between March and mid-May, has 36 bitterness units, and is crisp and quenching.

Einbecker Bräuhaus, Papen Strasse 4-7, 3352 Einbeck, Lower Saxony.

DOPPELBOCK

PAULANER DOPPELBOCK

Bock beer came south in the 17th century when a Duke of Brunswick married the daughter of a Bavarian noble in Munich. A century later an *Oanbock bier* was being produced in Munich's royal court brewery, the *Hofbräuhaus. Beck* became *Bock*, which was fortuitous as *Bock* also means a Billy Goat, a symbol much used on beer labels as a sign of potency and strength. *Doppelbock* means Double Bock: these beers are not necessarily twice as strong as a Bock but the term stresses the link with the "liquid bread" beers once made by Munich monks to sustain them during Lent. Paulaner's Salvator is the classic of the style and the company has been allowed to incorporate the name in its title. The brewery was founded by monks in the early 17th century. In the 18th century a commercial brewer named Franz-Xaver Zacherl took over the brewery and began to develop the Salvator – Holy Father – beer.

Its success prompted other brewers to make *Doppelbocks* with "-or" at the end of their

PAULANER-THOMAS-
BRÄU
Münchener
Paulaner
bräu
Dunkel
Exportbier
Hell-Urtyp
Export
BRAUEREI-ABZUG
MÜNCHEN

Above
Father Barnabas was a former brewmaster at Paulaner and helped perfect its Doppelbock beer.
Opposite
EKU 28 is one of the world's strongest bottled beers.

names, such as Triumphator, Fortunator and Celebrator. Salvator, the benchmark for the style, is brewed from three malts and Hallertauer hops. It is lagered for around three months and has a deep brown colour. It has a big malty-fruity aroma with a good underpinning of hops, a yeasty, malt loaf palate and an intense finish packed with dark fruit, malt and hops. The Thomas in the company's name refers to a second brewery bought by Paulaner that no longer brews.
Paulaner-Salvator-Thomasbräu,
Hochstrasse 75, Munich 95.

Kulminator 28

As the name Kulminator suggests, this beer is a Double Bock but is brewed in a style known as Eisbock, unique to Kulmbach (a second brewery, Kulmbacher Reichelbräu, also makes an ice beer). Do not confuse these Bavarian specialities with the modish but short-lived products from Canada, Australia, Japan and the US. The German beers, as a result of long lagering, have great depth and complexity, not skunky aromas reminiscent of nail-polish remover. The EKU in the company name translates as the first – Erste – brewery in Kulmbach that was the result of a merger or Union of two smaller breweries in the town in 1872. Kulminator 28 is renamed EKU 28 for export and is one of the strongest lagers in the world, with 13.5 per cent abv. "28" derives from an old German system of measuring alcohol. The beer is made from local pale barley malt and Hersbrücker, Perle and Tettnanger hops. Bitterness units are around 30. There is some caramelization of the sugars in the brew kettle, giving the beer an amber glow. The beer is lagered for nine months and towards the end of the storage period ice forms in the lager tanks. Water freezes before alcohol and the ice crystals are removed, concentrating the alcohol.

EKU has a rich malt aroma, some citric fruitiness on the palate and a long, deep finish with alcohol dominating and balanced by fruit, malt and hops. The beer is claimed to be a cure for the common cold: it would certainly take your mind off one.

Erste Kulmbacher Union Brauerei AG, EKU-strasse, 1, 8650 Kulmbach.

SMOKED BEER
AECHT SCHLENKERLA RAUCHBIER

The smoked beers of the Bamberg region of Franconia in northern Bavaria are a potent link with brewing's past, when all malt was cured over wood fires and beers had a smoky aroma and palate. The classic producer of the style is Heller-Trum, which started life in the Schlenkerla tavern in 1678, when the beer was lagered in caves dug in surrounding hills. Demand for the beer forced the company to move to larger premises.

The current brewery yard is packed with beechwood logs. Inside, there is a smokehouse where the barley malt lies on a mesh above a beechwood fire. The copper brewhouse has open vessels for primary fermentation, followed by two months' lagering.

Opposite
The Schlenkerla Tavern – the spiritual home of Rauchbier since 1678 and still the best place to sample this Franconian speciality.

Rauchbier is 5 per cent abv with 29 to 32 units of bitterness. It is dark brown in colour and has an intense smoked malt aroma and palate with hints of delicate fruit and hops. The brewery also makes an autumn Bock and Helles: both have powerful hints of smoked malt. *Aecht* is a dialect word for "old" while *Schlenkerla* is a rude nickname for a former brewer who had long, ape-like arms.

Brauerei Heller-Trum Schlenkerla, 6 Dominikaner Strasse, 8600 Bamberg.

ENGLAND

England is the last major brewing country to produce a substantial amount of beer by the method of warm or top fermentation. In spite of the growth in sales of lager beer – most of it a poor imitation of the genuine article – around half of the beer made in England is ale, in the form of mild ale, pale ale or bitter, porter and stout, old ales, barley wines and such seasonal beers as winter warmers and harvest ales. Close to 20 per cent of ale comes in cask-conditioned or bottle-conditioned form.

Opposite *Vaux's Double Maxim, both then and now. A malty brown ale from the North-east of England.*

It is, indeed, a remarkable testimony to the determination of brewing craftsmen and beer drinkers to remain loyal to a method of brewing – in which beers leave the brewery in an unfinished form to condition in the cask in the pub cellar or in the bottle – that the rest of the world has consigned to the history books. Bottle-conditioned beers exist in other countries, Belgium and Germany in particular, but only in England, and to a lesser extent in Scotland and Wales, do millions of gallons of beer mature inside casks, throw a yeast sediment and are served without extraneous gas pressure.

This is not to suggest that English brewing exists in some medieval time-warp. Pale ale, better known as bitter today, was as much a product of the industrial revolution as the lager beers of Munich, Pilsen and Vienna. In fact, it predated them by several decades. India Pale

Ale was brewed first for the colonial trade and was a major style throughout the world until it was supplanted by German lagers. IPA was synonymous with the brewing town of Burton on Trent in the Midlands where the hard, gypsum-rich spring waters encourage the production of flinty, star-bright, hoppy-fruity pale beers. The first pale ales were truly light in colour from just pale malt and brewing sugar but the use of crystal malt from the turn of the century gave the style its now familiar burnished copper colour.

While draught bitter or bottled pale ale is the dominant beer today, such older styles as porter and stout, old ales and barley wines survive and even proliferate as craft brewers widen their portfolios to please the growing number of connoisseurs searching for character and depth of flavour in their ales.

BROWN ALE

DOUBLE MAXIM

This is a robust example of the brown ales brewed in North-east England: the sweeter and less characterful Newcastle Brown Ale is the best-known version of the style.

The curious name stems from the military activities of Captain Ernest Vaux with a Maxim machine gun during the Boer War. His family-owned brewery honoured him on his return in 1901 with a beer called Maxim. Its strength was increased in the 1930s and the beer was renamed Double Maxim. It is 4.2 per cent abv and is brewed from a blend of pale and crystal malts with a touch of caramel for colour and is primed with sugar. Only Fuggles hops are used, creating 22 units of bitterness. The beer has an earthy Fuggles aroma, is rich and nutty in the mouth and becomes dry in the finish with some tart orange fruit.

Vaux Breweries, The Brewery, Sunderland SR1 3AN.

Pale Ale

Broadside

Broadside commemorates a battle between the English and Dutch fleets off the coast of the small coastal town of Southwold in East Anglia, the great barley-producing region of England. Adnams is a small, family-owned company, founded in 1872, whose beers have won acclaim and many prizes as a result of a determination to stick to traditional recipes and a refusal to cut corners where quality is concerned. Brewing takes place in superb copper mash tuns, brew kettles and high-sided wooden fermenters. The company has stayed loyal to England's finest and juiciest malting

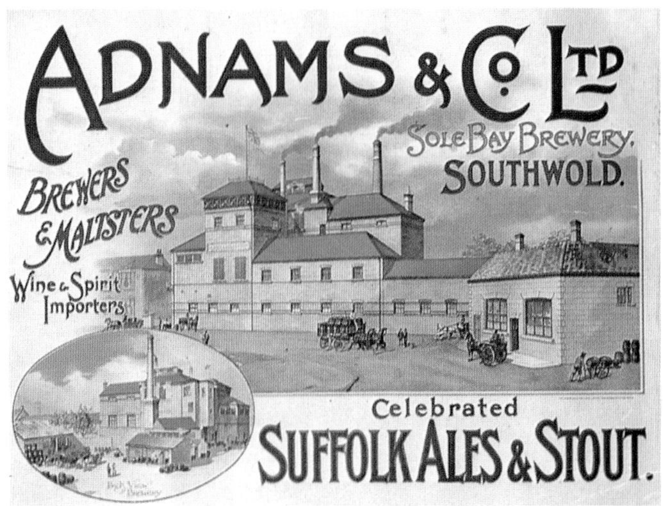

barley strain, Maris Otter, and to Fuggles and Goldings hops for their spicy and peppery aromas and tart bitterness. There is also some crystal malt and a touch of caramel in Broadside, a 4.8 per cent abv ale with 36 units of bitterness. It has a powerful spicy hops aroma with the tart orange fruit that is the hallmark of the brewery's yeast strain. Sweet malt and peppery hops blend in the mouth and the big finish is dominated by hops and quenching fruit. Is it the proximity of the North Sea a few yards from the brewery that gives Adnams' ales a hint of salt and seaweed?

Adnams & Co, Sole Bay Brewery, East Green, Southwold IP18 6JW.

Opposite
A classic pale ale from Adnams in Suffolk.

Above
The proximity of the North Sea to the brewery adds a dash of salt and seaweed to the flavours.

Right
Worthington's Brewery in Burton on Trent , home of pale ale. The company merged with Bass in the 1920s.
Opposite
Worthington White Shield, a heady reminder of the original India Pale Ales of the 19th century.

WORTHINGTON WHITE SHIELD

This is the nearest we are likely to get to the taste of the first India Pale Ales. Worthington was one of the great innovating Burton breweries which merged with its neighbour Bass in the 1920s. White Shield is a direct descendant of the first pale ales developed for the colonial trade in cask and bottle. It is by far the biggest-selling bottle-conditioned ale in Britain and comes complete with advice on how to pour it to keep the sediment of yeast in the bottle. It is 5.6 per cent

abv and is brewed from a blend of Halcyon and Pipkin pale malts. The merest hint of black malt is occasionally added to adjust the colour of the pale malts. Challenger and Northdown hops create a massive 40 units of bitterness. At the end of primary fermentation, the beer is filtered and then bottled with a dosage of priming sugar and a different yeast strain that acts more like a bottom-fermenter than a top one: it falls rapidly to the bottom of the bottle and turns the remaining sugars into alcohol.

The finished beer has spices, peppery hops, light fruit and a whiff of sulphur on the nose, with malt, hops and spices in the mouth and a nutty finish with hops dominating and some light apple fruit notes.
Bass Brewers, Cape Hill Brewery, PO Box 27, Birmingham B16 0PQ.

BLACK SHEEP BITTER

Black Sheep is a proud brewery producing excellent ales but there is a joke at the heart of its name. Masham is best known as the home of Theakston's Brewery, while Black Sheep is run by a certain Paul Theakston. When Theakston's was bought by the Scottish & Newcastle group, Paul left the brewery and eventually opened his own plant in a former maltings and just a few yards from the rival company. As he racked his brains for a name for his brewery, his wife commented: "You'll be the black sheep of the family now!" and his problem was solved. Black Sheep opened in the early 1990s and quickly established a name for the quality of its beers and its adherence to Yorkshire methods of production. In particular Paul was determined to ferment in traditional Yorkshire "squares", two-storey vessels in which the fermenting wort rises from the bottom to the top chamber and returns to the lower one, leaving yeast behind.

It is a time-honoured method of cleansing pale ale of yeast and helps produce the creamy head and texture with a noticeably hoppy aroma that is typical of the style. Black Sheep Bitter is 3.8 per cent abv. It is brewed from Maris Otter malt with crystal malt, torrefied wheat and a minute amount of roasted malt. The hops are Fuggles, Goldings and Progress. The beer has a powerful attack of Fuggles on the nose and a nutmeg spiciness, with more peppery hops in the mouth and a long finish that is a fine balance between creamy malt and bitter hops. *Black Sheep Brewery, Wellgarth, Masham, Ripon HG4 4EN*

Opposite & below *The oldest brewery in Yorkshire, Sam Smith's, and one of the newest, Paul Theakston's Black Sheep. Both produce excellent bottled ales that adhere to time-honoured Yorkshire traditions.*

OLD BREWERY PALE ALE

Sam Smith's Brewery is as ancient as Black Sheep is new. It is the oldest brewery in Yorkshire, founded in 1758 in the small town of Tadcaster – known as the "Burton of the North". The brewhouse is firmly traditional with conventional mash tuns and coppers, and square fermenters made of Welsh slate. The notion of installing modern stainless steel squares – as one leading Yorkshire brewery has done – would be anathema to Sam Smith's, which still employs coopers to fashion its wooden casks and makes local deliveries by horse-drawn drays. But the company is not lost in the past. It is conscious of modern drinkers'

Opposite *Spitfire Ale is bottle conditioned and comes from Shepherd Neame, the oldest brewery in England, dating back to 1698.*

demands and has phased out the use of brewing sugars except in some of its dark beers where sugar is an important contributor to flavour. Old Brewery Pale Ale is 5 per cent abv and is brewed from pale and crystal malts with Fuggles and Goldings hops. It has a spicy and peppery hop aroma balanced by ripe malt, with tart fruit, hops and cobnuts in the mouth, and a big malty-hoppy finish with hints of oak and vanilla. It is an enormously complex and characterful ale. Sam Smith's has a fine range of bottled beers: for information about its porter and stouts see the companion book, *Classic Stout and Porter.*

Samuel Smith Old Brewery, High Street, Tadcaster LS24 9SB.

SPITFIRE ALE

Shepherd Neame – "Sheps" for short – is Britain's oldest brewery, opened in 1698. It has unlined teak mash tuns dating from the First World War while a steam engine from the 17th century is still on view. The brewery is in the heart of the Kent hop fields and its ales have a noticeably tangy bitter character from such local varieties as Goldings and Target. Even the standard draught bitter, Master Brew, has a powerful 37 bitterness units while Spitfire notches 41. Spitfire is a recent addition to the range, launched to help raise funds for the Royal Air Force benevolent fund: RAF Spitfires played a memorable role during the Battle of

Britain in the Second World War in the skies over Kent. The success of the beer on draught encouraged Sheps to produce a bottle-conditioned version. It is 4.7 per cent abv and is made from Halcyon pale malt, crystal malt and some cereal adjuncts. It has a booming aroma of citric fruit, rich malt and hops, with full-bodied malt in the mouth and a long bitter finish packed with hops and citric fruit. Sheps also bottles Bishops Finger (5.2 per cent), a malty, nutty, fruity strong pale ale named after a Kentish road sign shaped like a finger.

Shepherd Neame, 17 Court Street, Faversham ME13 7AX.

Stout and Porter

Burton Porter

Burton Porter seems like a contradiction in terms. Burton is the home of pale ale brewing and was never a major centre for porter and stout. But Burton Bridge, based on the bridge over the River Trent that leads into the town, has produced a splendid revivalist porter, a fine example of the beer style that changed the face of British brewing in the 18th century. The small micro-brewery's products can be enjoyed in the Victorian Bridge Inn that forms part of the enterprise. Bridge Porter is available in both cask- and bottle-conditioned form. It is 4.5 per cent abv and is brewed from Pipkin pale, crystal and chocolate malts, with Challenger and Target hops. The colour is a deep ruby red edging towards mahogany, confirming that the early porters, unlike modern stouts, were not jet black. The aroma is a balance of light hops, chocolate and dark fruit, with biscuity malt in the mouth and a finish dominated by dark grain and fruit until the hops take over in a late burst. Burton Bridge also produces a seasonal 5 per cent stout, in bottle as well as cask.

Burton Bridge Brewery, 24 Bridge Street, Burton on Trent DE14 1SY.

Russian Imperial Stout

This is not only a magnificent beer but an historic one also, a link with the hey-day of British brewing when its products were the

Opposite
Burton is famous for its pale ale but the local micro brews a rich and flavoursome porter that matures naturally in the bottle.

envy of the world and exported to all parts. In the 19th century many London brewers made strong stouts for export. The style became so popular in Russia that it was enjoyed in the Tsar's court and supplies were given to troops to both refresh them and help them recover from their war wounds.

The export stout brewed by Barclay Perkins in particular was given the royal seal of approval and was branded Russian Imperial. Barclay's agent in the Baltic, a Belgian named Le Coq, built a brewery in Estonia to supply the region.

Barclay Perkins became part of the Courage group which has now merged with Scottish & Newcastle. Russian Imperial Stout moved from the old Anchor Brewery in London, where it matured for a year in oak vessels, to John Smith's brewery in Yorkshire. It is 10 per cent abv, brewed from a complex grist of pale, amber and black malts with a little Pilsner malt and brewing sugar. An enormous amount of Target hops are used in the copper: around 24 pounds per barrel, four times the amount for an average English ale, creating 50 units of bitterness. The stout has an aroma of fresh leather, molasses and fennel, with bitter chocolate in the mouth and a big finish packed with bitter dark fruit and hops.

Opposite
Taking steppes to get a good beer...a 1930s advertisement for Barclay's Russian Stout, the illustrious antecedent of Courage's Russian Imperial Stout.

Russian Imperial is bottle conditioned and will improve over time: a 30 year-old version is long in the finish with not only great depth but a smoother, creamier note as the aromas and flavours meld together.

John Smith's releases each annual batch after just a short brewery conditioning and bottles should be laid down for at least three months before consuming.

Courage Brewing, John Smith's Magnet Brewery, Tadcaster LS24 9SA.

RUSSIAN STOUT

Matured at least a year in bottle—and goes on maturing

OLD ALE

STRONG SUFFOLK ALE

Old Ale originally meant a beer stored for a year or more in wooden vessels. During that long conditioning period the beer developed fruity, vinous and even lactic flavours. The beer, also known as "stale" in 18th-century England, was an important constituent of the earliest porters, known as "three threads", a blend of pale, brown and stale.

The best example of a blended ale with links to the earlier days of brewing is Greene King's Strong Suffolk. The 6 per cent abv beer is a blend of a 5 per cent BPA (Best Pale Ale) and Old 5X. The latter beer is 12 per cent and is matured in untreated oak vats for two years. The enormous casks, each one holding 60 barrels, are tucked away at the back of the brewery and are reached by narrow ladders and catwalks. The lids of the vats are covered with layers of Suffolk marl, the local chalky soil, to stop wild yeasts attacking the slumbering beer. Nevertheless, Old 5X, tasted straight in the brewery, does have a slight lactic sourness before blending that is still noticeable when mixed with the malty BPA. The finished beer has a rich fruity, oaky aroma and palate and a bitter, medicinal hint of quinine, with a peppery and spicy hop character from Challenger, Northdown and Target varieties. The beer has an affinity with Rodenbach's sour red ale in Belgium.

Greene King, Westgate Brewery, Bury St Edmunds IP33 1QT.

Opposite
Greene King's Strong Suffolk is a blend of two ales, one matured in oak tuns.
Below
Richard Gale, bought Gale's Brewery in 1847.

PRIZE OLD ALE

Here is a beer that proclaims quality and antiquity. It comes in hand-corked, sealed and numbered bottles, with a handsome label showing the brewery in Victorian times. It is brewed and fermented in old wooden vessels including some "rounds" – rare iron-hooped fermenters.

The brewery, with an old coaching inn attached, has survived two fires and the death of a head brewer who committed suicide by plunging into a vat of fermenting beer.

POA is 9 per cent abv and is brewed from Maris Otter malt and tiny amounts of black malt and wheat. Hops are Fuggles and Goldings. It has 47.5 units of bitterness. The beer is properly aged, as befits the name. It is stored for up to a year in tanks before being bottled without any addition of sugar or yeast. It will improve and deepen and increase in strength with age. It is reddish in colour with hops and apple fruit on the nose, malt, spices and fruit in the mouth, and a dry fruity finish with hints of raisins and apple. When aged the apple fruit takes on a Calvados-type character. A former head brewer – not the one who committed suicide – said the beer was at its best after 20 years.

George Gale & Co, The Brewery, Horndean, Portsmouth PO8 0DA.

THOMAS HARDY'S ALE

The brewery is the former Eldridge Pope plant that has now been hived off to run as a separate commercial concern. It is named after the gloomy Wessex novelist and poet Thomas Hardy as he knew the Pope family well and wrote glowingly of the ales of "Casterbridge", his name for Dorchester.

Thomas Hardy's Ale was brewed for a literary festival in 1968 and aroused such interest that it has been brewed regularly ever since. It is brewed from Pipkin pale malt only: the russet colour is the result of some caramelization of the brewing sugars during an extremely long copper boil. It is hopped with Challenger, Goldings and Northdown and dry hopped with Styrian Goldings. Bitterness units reach 75. The abv is a nominal 12 per cent that will increase in the bottle.

The beer comes in vintage-dated nip bottles. Drunk young, it is spicy, treacly and fruity. With a year or two under its belt it becomes rounder, fuller, more complex with hops peeping through the daunting layers of malt and alcohol. I have drunk vintages going back more than 20 years, with aromas and flavours reminiscent of fresh tobacco, old books and leather. It is a remarkable beer.

Thomas Hardy Brewery, Weymouth Avenue, Dorchester DT1 1QT.

Opposite
Gale's legendary old ale is sold in hand-corked bottles.
Above
Thomas Hardy's Ale is named after the writer who praised the beers of "Casterbridge" in his Wessex novels.

BARLEY WINE

NORMAN'S CONQUEST

The distinction between old ale and barley wine is a hazy one, especially in the case of Cottage's bottle-conditioned beer that will improve with ageing.

Historically, the difference was clear: old ale was matured for long periods while the term barley wine indicated the strongest beer produced in a brewery, with a strength similar to that of wine and perhaps even finished with a wine yeast, as conventional brewer's yeast struggles to produce more than 12 or 13 per cent abv: beers such as Boston Brewery's Triple Bock, around 19 per cent, are finished with champagne yeast. If 7 per cent seems a modest strength for a "malt wine" then think of white rather than of red.

Norman's Conquest – with a starting gravity of 1066, a nice touch of historical humour – won the coveted Champion Beer of Britain competition in 1995, quite a remarkable achievement for a beer up against mainstream milds and bitters. That was in draught form and the victory encouraged owner/brewer Chris Norman to produce a bottle-conditioned version, on the strength of which this tiniest of minnow breweries has gone from a 10-barrel to a 20-barrel plant.

Opposite
Eye, eye, it's a champion beer. Norman's Conquest was named Champion Beer of Britain in 1995.

The beer is brewed from pale, crystal and pale chocolate malts and is hopped entirely with Challenger. It has 34 units of bitterness, a

big peppery-spicy aroma balanced by rich malt, tart fruit, hops and chocolate in the mouth, and a long finish that becomes dry and is a complex mix of rich malt, dark vinous fruit and spicy hops.

Cottage Brewing Co., Little Orchard, High Street, West Lydford, Somerset TA11 7DQ.

GOLDEN PRIDE

At 9.2 per cent abv this is a redoubtable ale, one for sipping and savouring rather than quaffing. It is brewed by one of London's two remaining independent brewers, hard by the River Thames and famous for such prize-winning cask beers as London Pride and Extra Special Bitter.

The Fuller's house yeast imparts a noticeably fruity character to its beers and this is most apparent in Golden Pride, brewed from Alexis pale and crystal malts, with a complex hops grist of Challenger, Goldings, Northdown and Target. It is rich, rounded and bursting with ripe, tart fruit – Seville oranges leading the pack – with a firm underpinning of peppery hops. The finish is a brilliant balance of hops, fat grain and vinous fruit.

Each year a small amount of the beer is placed in wooden casks and matured for several months before being released on draught for Christmas. In the tradition of barley wines, the casks are regularly rolled round the brewery yard to encourage a good second fermentation.
Fuller, Smith & Turner, Griffin Brewery, Chiswick Lane South, London W4 2QB.

Opposite
Golden Pride is one of the clutch of splendid ales brewed by Fuller's in West London.
Below
Lees' Moonraker has been described as "sherry with hops".

MOONRAKER

The curious name comes from a bibulous fable which claims that when this area of Manchester was rural, farm labourers who had drunk rather too deeply of the local strong ale saw the reflection of the moon in a pond and attempted to capture it with their long-handled rakes.

This luscious 7.5 per cent abv ale is brewed only from Maris Otter pale malt and East Kent Goldings: the deep, burnished gold colour is the result of the large amount of malt and some deepening of colour during the copper boil.

John Willy Lees' house yeast gives an orange fruit character to all the beers and is most pronounced in Moonraker. Fruit, ripe malt and

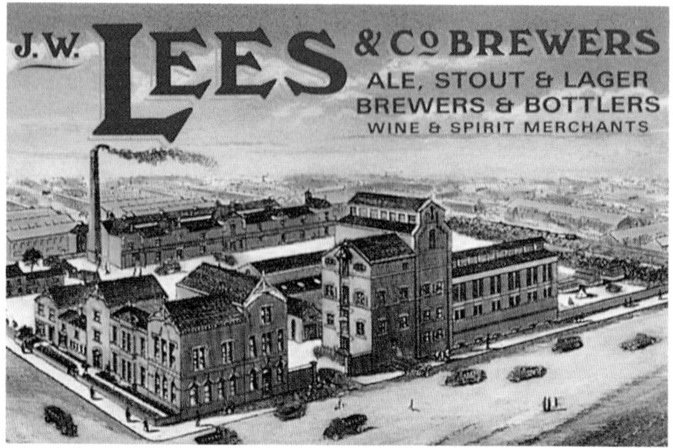

Opposite *A 1930s poster promoting the warming qualities of Robinson's Old Tom from Stockport.* ***Above*** *Lees' Brewery in Manchester. Its beers have a pronounced orange fruit character from the house yeast.*

massive peppery hops dominate the aroma with rich malt and hop prickle on the tongue and bitter-sweet finish with more orange fruit notes. The beer was once memorably described as being "like sherry with hops in it".

J W Lees, Greengate Brewery, Middleton Junction, Manchester M24 2AX.

Old Tom

The label carries a picture of a Tom cat, not perhaps the best image for a barley wine. But this sumptuous beer does not smell or taste remotely like a feline by-product. It is 8.5 per cent abv (should that be "purr cent"?) and is brewed from Halcyon and Pipkin pale malts, crystal, a small amount of flaked maize and torrefied wheat, with a touch of caramel for colour adjustment. Hops are Goldings with a small percentage of Northdown. The bottled

F. ROBINSON'S

Old Tom Ale

"Prevents those Winter Shivers"

TRADE MARK

beer is taken from a cask-conditioned version, which is dry hopped with Goldings. The family-owned Robinson's brewery is highly traditional and frowns upon such innovations as hop pellets – crushed and pressed into large green pills – and prefers the whole flowers. Old Tom has a heady, winey aroma of dark fruit, there is big juicy malt in the mouth balanced by peppery hops, and the finish is a balance of port-wine fruit and bitter hops. Drink it from a saucer.

Frederic Robinson, Unicorn Brewery, Hillgate, Stockport SK1 1JJ.

OLD NICK

The Devil has the best tunes – and the best beers. Old Nick was a sideline at Young's famous South London brewery, with its traditional brewing vessels, dray horses and ram mascot, until the company started to export some of its stronger beers.

The barley wine became something of a sensation in Scandinavia where beer drinkers are starved of strong beers. It is also popular in the United States though sales are slow in those states where the born-again bible brigade bridle at the powerful image of the epitome of all evil on the label. Young's has remained faithful to Maris Otter malting barley and blends this

with a large proportion of crystal malt. Hops are traditional Fuggles and Goldings, creating 50 to 55 units of bitterness. The 7.25 per cent abv beer is red-brown in colour, has a yeasty-biscuity aroma balanced by tart hops, with vinous fruit and hops in the mouth and a big bitter-sweet, hoppy-fruity finish.

Young & Co, The Ram Brewery, High Street, Wandsworth, London SW18 4JD.

Above
Young's Old Nick is a devil of a beer but raises passions in the Bible belt.

Opposite
An ancient bottle of Robinson's powerful ale.

Wales

Opposite & below
Double Dragon, from the Felinfoel Brewery, is a rich and malty ale firmly in the Welsh tradition and a racing certainty to please any drinker.

Double Dragon

Here is a Welsh classic, a masterpiece from a country that has lost most of its breweries and much of its brewing tradition. Felinfoel – pronounced *Vell-in-voi-el* – is a family-owned company that flies the ale flag proudly with malt accented beers.

At 4.2 per cent abv, Double Dragon (sold in the US as Welsh Ale), is brewed from Pipkin pale malt, crystal malt and brewing sugar. Bramling Cross, Challenger and Whitbread Goldings Variety hops produce 25 units of bitterness. It has a rich, ripe malty aroma with delicate hop notes, malt and vinous fruit in the mouth, and a long finish packed with tart fruit, some toffee notes and spicy hops.

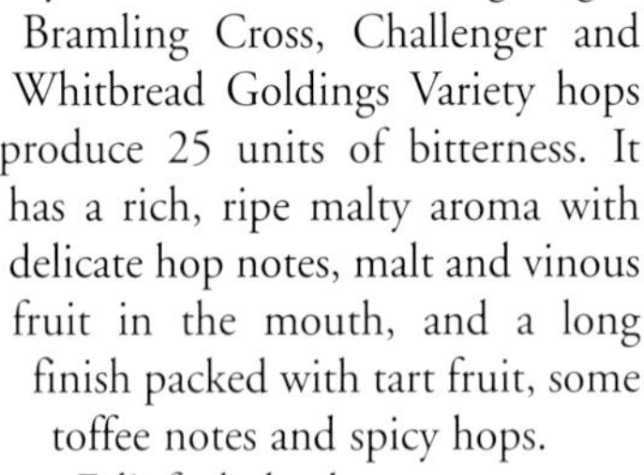

Felinfoel also brews a now rare example of Dark, the mild ales that once refreshed legions of miners and steel workers in the Welsh valleys. As a result of its connections with the tin-plate industry, Felinfoel has the dubious distinction of being the first brewery to can beer in the 1930s.

Felinfoel Brewery, Farmers Row, Felinfoel, Llanelli SA14 8LB.

DRINK
FELINFOEL ALES
"an easy first"
A TIP
from the Old Firm
THE FELINFOEL BREWERY C^O L^TD
LLANELLY

SCOTLAND

Scotland shares with England a brewing tradition based on top-fermenting ales. But there is a sharp difference in the style brewed north of the border. As there is no local hop industry, the plant has been used more sparingly in Scottish ales. As a result they tend to be more heavily malt-accented than English ales and are often more rounded from the use of darker malts. It is part of the tradition of Scottish brewing that generous amounts of crystal, roast, chocolate and black malts are used, producing beers with rich bitter-sweet roasted and chocolate character.

Scotland is a cold country and beers have to provide internal central heating as well as refreshment. The appearance of a clutch of small craft brewers has added immeasurably to the pleasures of drinking.

Scottish stouts – sharply different to the dry Irish style – 70 and 80 shilling ales (named after a 19th-century method of invoicing beer based on strength) and golden IPAs have made welcome revivals. At Traquair House in the Borders you can visit a medieval working brewery offering a powerful ale as well as a glimpse of brewing's past.

Opposite
Coopers at the Lorimer & Clark Brewery in Edinburgh – now known as the Caledonian.

ST ANDREW'S ALE

Belhaven Brewery is just a stone's throw from the border with England but it wears its tartan with pride. St Andrew's Ale commemorates the

Opposite *Belhaven's St Andrew's ale commemorates a famous Scottish victory over the English.* ***Above*** *Belhaven is based in buildings that were once a maltings and date from 1719.*

hero of a battle with the English. It is one of several magnificent ales brewed in buildings that once formed a maltings. The brewery dates from 1719 but there are records showing that a monastic brewhouse stood on the site in the 14th century. Belhaven resurrected the style of Scottish ale that rises in strength from 60 shilling to 90 shilling: "60 Bob" is equivalent to an English mild while 90 shilling is similar to a warming old ale. Its 80 Shilling, with its tart and pungent gooseberry fruitiness, is the classic of the style. St Andrew's Ale (4.5 per cent abv) is brewed from Pipkin pale malt with black and crystal for colour and body. Fuggles and Goldings create 36 units of bitterness, high by Scottish standards. The beer is also dry hopped in cask before bottling, which adds to the hop bitterness. The aroma is a rich blend of tart fruit from the house yeast and peppery/spicy

hops, with full malt and cobnuts from the crystal in the mouth, and a lingering bitter-sweet, hoppy-fruity, beautifully balanced finish.
Belhaven Brewery, Spott Road,
Dunbar EH42 1RS.

OLD JOCK

Broughton is a small brewery in the Scottish Borders founded by David Younger, a member of one half of the famous Scottish brewing dynasty, McEwan and Younger, that formed Scottish & Newcastle Breweries. The main beer from Broughton is Greenmantle Ale, named in honour of John Buchan, who came from the village and wrote the famous gung-ho adventures of Richard Hannay.

Old Jock is a strong ale that hovers, perhaps as a result of the closeness of the English border, between an old ale and a Scottish "wee heavy". It is 6.7 per cent abv and is brewed from pale malt

and roasted barley, the dark grain giving it a fine burnished copper colour. Fuggles and Goldings create 32 units of bitterness. The beer has spicy and vinous aromas, rounded malt, fruit and butterscotch dominate the mouth and the finish is bitter-sweet with dark raisin fruit and a good underpinning of peppery hops and an enticing spiciness.

In the past the beer was re-labelled for sale in the United States for fear Americans thought Old Jock was a form of sportsman's underwear used in the brewing process.

Broughton Brewery, Broughton,
Biggar ML12 6HQ.

Above
Broughton's Greenmantle is named after the writer John Buchan who lived in the village.
Opposite
Old Jock is spicy and vinous and isn't strained through sportsmen's underwear.

DEUCHAR'S IPA & GOLDEN PROMISE

The Caledonian Brewery in Edinburgh is one of the finest in Britain. It began life curiously as a Scottish brewery set up to supply the North-east of England rather than local markets. It was based next to the Caledonian Railway that ran from the Scots capital to Newcastle upon Tyne and Sunderland and specialised in a style of creamy-malty ale known confusingly as Scotch.

When the owners announced the closure of the brewery in 1987 it was rescued by a management buy-out. It is now revered for the quality of its ales, which include 60, 70 and 80 shilling ales and amber and porter beers. R&D Deuchar's IPA (3.8 per cent abv) is a classic interpretation of the style as it was developed in Scotland. Edinburgh, with hard water similar to Burton upon Trent's, followed the English brewers to the colonies with India Pale Ale in the 19th century.

Deuchar's is a long-closed brewery but Russell Sharp, managing director of "the Caley", has revived the recipe. Using Pipkin pale and crystal malt and a small amount of wheat malt, with Fuggles and Goldings hops, he has produced a golden ale with 35 units of bitterness, a distinctive earthy Goldings nose with tart citric fruit notes, a quenching balance of malt and hops in the mouth and a lingering hoppy/fruity finish. It has won a host of prizes at CAMRA beer festivals.

Golden Promise (5 per cent) is a rarity, an ale brewed only from organic materials, including Scottish barley malt and English organic hops.

Even by English standards, with 50 to 52 units of bitterness, this is a bitter beer. It has a pronounced malt and floral hops aroma, with orange fruit dominating the palate and a deep and complex finish with citric fruit, biscuity malt and spicy hops.

Caledonian Brewing Company, Slateford Road, Edinburgh EH11 1PH.

Opposite
Caledonian has won many prizes for its Deuchar's IPA, a faithful recreation of the 19th-century style. Golden Promise is that rarity, a beer brewed from organic ingredients.

FRAOCH HEATHER ALE

Fraoch – pronounced "frook" – is a link with one of the oldest brewing methods in the world. The first brewers in Scotland were not Celts, from whom modern Scots are descended, but cave-dwelling Picts. The Picts were massacred in the 4th century but their verbal recipe for heather ale was passed on by word-of-mouth and was still being brewed in isolated areas in the 18th century.

In 1993 Bruce Williams, a home-brewer, discovered that a woman in the remote Western Isles had translated a recipe for the style from

Opposite *Maclay of Alloa has revived the old Scottish style of Oatmalt Stout, a creamy and smooth dark beer quite distinct from the dry Irish style.*
Above *Bruce Williams found a recipe so old it was never written down but passed on by word of mouth in Gaelic. Fraoch Ale uses heather as well as barley malt.*

Gaelic into English. Williams brewed a heather ale from the recipe and found he had a minor sensation on his hands. He has refined and refashioned the beer since and now has it brewed for him by Maclay of Alloa.

He uses 12 litres per barrel of bell and ling varieties of heather: half the heather goes into the copper and the remainder lines the hop back and acts as a filter for the hopped wort when it leaves the copper. Heather makes up a quarter of the total grist of the beer. The other ingredients are Scotch ale malt, carapils and wheat malt, 100 grammes of ginger root and Brewers Gold hops. The 5 per cent abv beer has an earthy heather and herbal aroma with a hint of fennel, a dry herbal palate with orange fruit and a finish that becomes dry and minty. Dr Keith Thomas of the Brewer's Laboratory, Sunderland University, carried out research into heather and discovered it contains a white

powder known as fog that includes micro-organisms that aid fermentation and would have acted spontaneously when heather ale was brewed without cultured yeast centuries ago.
Heather Ale, 736 Dumbarton Road, Glasgow G11 6RD.

MACLAY OATMALT STOUT

Alloa once vied with Edinburgh for the title of Brewing Capital of Scotland. There are just two breweries left: a Carlsberg-Tetley plant making mainly lager and processed beer, and Maclay.

Maclay, founded in 1830, is both fiercely traditional and independent, using superb old mash tuns, coppers and open fermenting vessels to craft a wide variety of ales, ranging from a dark 60 Shilling through a porter to an Old Ale. Perhaps its major contribution to Scottish beer is the revivalist Oatmalt Stout, a style that was once a mainstay of most brewery portfolios but which had fallen from grace. It is a beer firmly in the Scottish mould, creamy, rich and rounded, in sharp distinction to the Irish style of stout. Maclay's stout is 4.5 per cent abv and is brewed from Maris Otter pale malt, malted oats, roast barley and chocolate malt. Fuggles hops help create 35 units of bitterness. Malted oats account for 22 per cent of the grist, a surprisingly high amount as oats tend to gelatinize and are a difficult grain to brew with. They give to the beer a

Opposite Traquair House Ale is a potent brew made in a restored medieval brewhouse.
Right *Skullsplitter recalls the exploits of the Vikings who, in their time, were legendary quaffers of strong ale.*

creamy and delectably chewy note alongside rich hops and roasted barley on the aroma, a malty sweetness in the mouth and a bitter-sweet finish with tart hops and chocolate.
Maclay & Company, Thistle Brewery, Alloa FK10 1ED.

SKULLSPLITTER

Skullsplitter is not the promise of a hangover but an historic reference to a genuine Thorfin Skullsplitter, 7th Viking Earl of Orkney.

The Orkney Brewery, founded in 1987 in a derelict schoolhouse, is now such a success that owner Roger White has moved to mainland Scotland to run the sales side of the company while brewing continues on Orkney. White is an Englishman, a civil engineer who conceived the idea of running a micro-brewery while he was working in the "dry" Arab Gulf States. Skullsplitter, with a terrifying Viking on the label, is 8.5 per cent abv and is brewed with Golden Promise Scottish malt, crystal and chocolate malts and torrefied wheat. Whitbread Goldings Variety (actually a Fuggle-derivative) and Goldings are used and create 20 units of bitterness. The beer has a powerful fruity-winey aroma, with smooth, satiny malt in the mouth and a deceptively light, dry finish with rich fruit notes.

Roger White has also experimented with a Bere Ale using a pre-historic variety of barley still grown on Orkney and used for milling and in oatcakes.

Orkney Brewery, Quoyloo, Sandwick, Orkney KW16 3LT.

TRAQUAIR HOUSE ALE

Traquair House, in the hauntingly beautiful Borders countryside, is the oldest inhabited stately building in Scotland. Mary Queen of Scots stayed there frequently and Prince Charles Edward Stuart – Bonnie Prince Charlie, leader of the Jacobite rebellion – was a visitor. The house is owned by the Maxwell Stuarts and they keep the main Bear Gates closed

Opposite *Traquair House is Scotland's oldest inhabited house. Mary Queen of Scots stayed there, as did Bonnie Prince Charlie.*

until a Stuart returns to the throne. The former laird of the estate, Peter Maxwell Stuart, discovered a disused Elizabethan brewhouse in a stable block in the grounds. He restored it and started to brew ale with the help of a legendary Scots brewer, Sandy Hunter of Belhaven. The 7.2 per cent abv beer is something of a cult drink in the United States and Japan as well as at home.

Since Peter Maxwell Stuart's death, the house and brewery are administered by his daughter Catherine and a professional brewer. The beer is brewed from pale malt with the tiniest touch of black. East Kent Goldings are supplied by the specialist grower Tony Redsell from his farm in faraway Kent. The ale has a spicy and hoppy aroma with a hint of chocolate, there is rich vinous fruit in the mouth and the finish is dominated by hops, pineapple fruit and chocolate. Their Jacobite Ale (8 per cent), based on a house recipe from the 1690s, has a rich, warm, biscuity aroma balanced by hops and a herbal note from the addition of coriander. There is tart fruit in the mouth and the bitter-sweet finish has hints of chocolate, winey fruit and coriander. A draught Bear Ale (5 per cent) can be enjoyed in the nearby Traquair Arms in Innerleithen village.

The house and brewery are open to visitors in spring, summer and early autumn.
Traquair House, Innerleithen,
near Peebles EH44 6PW.

Ireland

Opposite
Beamish is the oldest brewer of stout in the Irish Republic, founded by two beef barons from the north of the island.

Ireland is synonymous with stout. Though porter and stout were first developed in London in the early 18th century, the style spread to Ireland and was taken up with such enthusiasm by the likes of Arthur Guinness in Dublin and Beamish & Crawford in Cork that they stopped production of pale ales in order to concentrate on dark beers.

Irish stout became a distinctive style in its own right in the 19th century when Guinness started to blend some unmalted roasted barley with malted grains. At the time malt was taxed and Guinness used some unmalted grain in order to pay less duty to the British rulers of Ireland. The roasty, bitter chocolate and dry fruit character added to the beer prompted other Irish stout brewers to follow Guinness's lead. When restrictions where placed on dark malt production in Britain during World War One to conserve energy, the Irish had the market to themselves. Porter was eventually phased out by the Irish brewers in order to concentrate on the stronger stout. Guinness became and remains the biggest supplier of stout to the British market and is now a vast international group. Both Beamish and Murphy, owned by large international drinks companies, are also busily expanding sales.

In spite of the growth of lager in Ireland and the survival of pockets of ale brewing, half the beer produced in Ireland is still stout. What is seen as a sideline in other countries, a footnote in brewing history, is inextricably linked in Ireland with its history, culture and nationhood.

BEAMISH STOUT

Beamish & Crawford claims to be the oldest surviving brewer of stout in Ireland. They were producing porter by 1792, several years before Arthur Guinness stopped brewing ale to concentrate on porter. Messrs William Beamish and William Crawford, of Scottish Protestant descent, came from the north of Ireland to sell butter and beef, saw the vast amounts of London and Bristol porter coming in through the port of Cork and decided to brew porter themselves. They bought an old ale brewery and quickly refashioned it as the Cork Porter Brewery.

The business was very successful and for a time was the biggest brewer in the whole of the United Kingdom of Great Britain and Ireland, producing 100,000 barrels a year, compared to Guinness's 66,000. But Beamish's sales were hit badly by the Irish famine in the 1840s and the dramatic decline in population caused by death and emigration, and it never recovered. In common with its competitors, Beamish has

phased out porter and concentrates on stout. The brewery, now part of the Scottish Courage group, has a substantial presence in Britain. Beamish Stout (4.3 per cent abv) is brewed from pale and dark malts, malted wheat, roast barley and wheat syrup and is hopped with Irish Northdown, German Hallertauer and Perle, and Styrian Goldings. It has 38 to 44 units of bitterness. The aroma is hoppy and chocolatey, grainy and fruity in the mouth, with a deep, bitter-sweet finish underscored by generous hop bitterness.

Beamish & Crawford, The Counting House, South Main Street, Cork.

GUINNESS FOREIGN EXTRA STOUT

There are more than 19 versions of Guinness stout brewed world-wide today and of them Foreign Extra Stout – FES for short – is the most fascinating. It is a palpable link with the early days of porter brewing and was developed by Arthur Guinness II in the 19th century for sale to British colonies in order to rival the India Pale Ales of the Burton brewers. It was first known as Foreign Extra Porter Stout but the word "porter" was eventually phased out from the label.

Tucked away in the vast modern, stainless steel Dublin brewery are two old oak vats dating from Arthur Guinness's first brewery from the mid-18th century. Stout is stored in the vats for one to three months where it picks up lactic flavours from the action of wild Brettanomyces yeasts. This is "stale beer" in the historic meaning of the word. It is blended with young stout and the bottles are then stored for a further month before they are released for sale. FES is 7.5 per cent abv and is made from pale malt, flaked barley and 10 per cent unmalted roasted barley. Hops are a blend of Galena, Nugget and Target, creating bitterness units in

Opposite
The impressive site of the Beamish & Crawford plant in Cork. Once the biggest brewery in the whole of the British Isles.

Above
A 19th century showcard for bottled Guinness. Draught Guinness is now dominant in the British Isles but the more complex bottled versions are still favoured in parts of Africa and the Caribbean.

the 60s. The complex stout has a toasty, roasty, winey and woody aroma, a full bitter-sweet palate with great hop character and a finish that becomes dry and bitter with hints of sour fruit. There are further hints of liquorice and dark and mysterious fruits. And on the nose there is the unmistakable aroma that brewers call "horse blanket" from the action of wild yeasts.
Arthur Guinness & Son, St James's Gate Brewery, Dublin 8.

Murphy's Irish Stout

The Murphy brothers James, William, Jerome and Frances, who had made their fortunes as grain merchants and whiskey distillers, opened their brewery in 1856 as Catholic competition to Beamish & Crawford. The plant was built on the site of an orphan's hospital, with a consecrated well that figures in the company title, though "holy water" has never been used for brewing.

The brewery was instantly successful and built up considerable sales in the United States among the expatriate Irish community where the name Murphy had, and still has, great resonance. The company is now part of the Heineken group, which gives the Irish stout considerable presence in world markets. Heineken's links with the Whitbread group means that Murphy's has been able to build a solid base in Britain. (The draught Murphy's Irish Stout sold in Britain is actually brewed in Wales: a Welsh Irish Stout could be the ultimate Irish joke.)

Perhaps it is the Heineken influence that makes Murphy's the most easily drinkable of the three Irish stouts but perhaps less characterful than its rivals' beers. It is 4.3 per cent abv with 35 to 36 units of bitterness. The ingredients are pale and chocolate malts with roasted barley, and all Target hops. It is quenching, lightly fruity and roasty, creamy and chocolatey in the mouth and with a dry and slightly fruity finish. See the companion title in the series, *Classic Stout and Porter.*

Murphy's, Lady's Well Brewery,
Leitrim Street, Cork.

The Netherlands

Opposite
Brand Pils and the Bock-style Imperator. The Koninklijke brewery is the oldest commercial brewery in the Netherlands dating back to the 14th century.

The Netherlands lives under the giant beery shadow cast by Heineken. The internationally famous Grolsch is a big brewing concern but it is tiny compared to the all-conquering giant in Amsterdam. But choice is slowly beginning to improve as a few small craft breweries, encouraged by the choice and awesome tradition of neighbouring Belgium, attempt to bring some diversity to Dutch drinkers. There are some quality Pilsner-style beers and few top-fermenting varieties that recall the time when ale was drunk and exported widely before Gerard Adriaan Heineken changed the face of beer in 1863 at his Haystack Brewery. Some of the revivalist beers, such as the astonishing ales in the 't IJ and Maximiliaan brewpubs in Amsterdam, and even Dutch versions of spontaneous fermentation, require a visit to drink them on draught but several specialist brews are now finding their way into bottle. And the Netherlands is also home to the sixth of the Trappist breweries in the Low Countries near Tilburg.

Brand Pils and Brand-UP

Koninklijke means the Royal Brewery as the company was appointed as official purveyor to the Dutch monarchy in the 1970s. The Pils is sold in the United States as Royal Brand Beer. It is the oldest commercial brewery in the Netherlands and dates from the early 14th

century in a village near Maastricht. The present site was built in 1743 and the brewery switched to lager production with enthusiasm in the 19th century. It became part of the Heineken group in 1989 but is given considerable autonomy. This independence of spirit is shown by the brewery's opposition to pasteurization. The head brewer declares: "Pasteurization serves to lengthen the shelf-life of beer but only marginally and at enormous cost to the taste and aroma of beer". Brand Pils is 5 per cent abv and is brewed from pale malt with 10 per cent maize. Hops are Northern Brewer, Hersbrücker and Perle, achieving 26 to 28 units of bitterness. The beer is lagered for 42 days and has a perfumy hop aroma, a firm malty body balanced by hops, and a long, delicate hoppy-malty finish. The 5.5 per cent Brand-UP is not a variation on an American soft drink but is a premium Pilsner: UP stands for *Urtyp Pilsner* – Original Pilsner. It is an all-malt brew and is hopped with Hersbrücker, Spalt and Tettnanger varieties and has an impressive 36 to 38 bitterness units. It is a delight to drink, with its enticing and aromatic nose of floral hops and tart lemon fruit, a bitter-sweet palate and lingering citric finish. Brand also brews a German-style Bock called Imperator (7 per cent).

Koninklijke Brand Bierbrouwerij BV, Postbus 1, 6300 AA Wijlre.

Budels Alt

Budel is an energetic independent brewery founded in 1870 near the Belgian border in the Dutch region of Brabant. It began with standard Pils-type lagers but has recently branched out with some more characterful beers, including top-fermenting ales with intriguing names. Parel, for example, means Pale Ale, while Capucijn is an abbey-style ale named after a monk's cowl (this is also the source of the name cappuccino). Alt is a rather more direct name and pays bibulous homage to the great ale style of nearby Düsseldorf in Germany. It is 5.5 per cent abv, brewed from pale and dark malts, and hopped with German varieties. It has massive peppery hops on the nose, dark chocolate and malt in the mouth, and a deep, dry and intensely bitter finish, with some fruit and coffee. It is a big beer in every way and would surprise German drinkers used to the more restrained character of their Altbiers.

Budelse Brouwerij, Nieuwstraat 9, 6021 HP Budel.

Opposite
Colourful labels stress the character of Budel beer. The Alt is a big-bodied interpretation of the Düsseldorf style across the border in Germany.
Left
Grolsch has achieved international cult status as a result of the quality of the Pils-style beer and the quaint "swing-top" bottle.

GROLSCH PILS

Let's get the confusion out of the way first: the beer is called Grolsch, the company is Grolsche and both derive from the ancient town of Grolle, now known as Groenlo, in the region of Gelderland. The company's Pils – labelled Premium Lager in some export markets – became a cult beer in the late 1970s and early 1980s as a result of its swing-top stoppered bottle, now much-copied. The Gelderlanders have a reputation, like the Scots, of being careful with their cash and they like the stoppered bottles because they can re-seal them rather than having to drink an entire bottle in one session. When Grolsche attempted to phase out the swing-top, the locals demanded its retention and helped launch an international success. The Pils is brewed from malts from Belgium, England, France, Germany and the Netherlands, with a small amount of maize, and hopped with Hallertauer and Saaz varieties. It is lagered for 10 weeks, has 27 bitterness units and is not pasteurized. As a result, it has a delightfully fresh aroma like new-mown grass, with citric fruit in the mouth and a long, delicate finish with bitter-sweet malt and hop notes. Grolsche also produces an Alt-style beer called Amber, an Oud Bruin and a Bock.

Grolsche Bierbrouwerij, Eibergseweg 10, 7141 CE Groenlo.

LA TRAPPE

Opposite
The Sheepfold Brewery in the grounds of the Trappist monastery at Koningshoeven near Tilburg.

For years the monks at Koningshoeven near Tilburg were the sole brewers of ales in the Netherlands. The brewery was opened in 1884 at the abbey whose name means King's Gardens: the land was given to the Trappists by the Dutch king in order to found their abbey when they migrated north from France. The Schaapskoi (sheepfold) brewery was set up to help raise funds for the restoration of the abbey. After World War Two the brewery was bought by Stella Artois, which wanted to build a

bridgehead in the Netherlands. Its unlikely "Trappist Pils" flopped and the monks bought back the plant and began brewing again. The brewing plant today is modern and stainless steel but the bottle-conditioned ales it produces are magnificent. After years of confusing labelling, they are all branded La Trappe today. The beers are brewed from blends of pale, Munich and coloured malts, with Hallertauer and English Goldings hops. La Trappe Dubbel (6.5 per cent abv) has a tawny appearance with a superb Muscat grape aroma and palate underscored by peppery hops. The 8 per cent Tripel has an enormous earthy Goldings aroma and spicy palate and finish. Quadrupel (10 per

cent) is an autumn vintage, reddish in colour with a smooth palate that belies the rich alcohol. The Trappist brothers have also launched a pale Enkel of 5.5 per cent which is dry, quenching and hoppy, a competitor to Chimay White and Orval. *Koningshoeven Trappistenbierbrouwerij de Schaapskoi, Eindhovensweg 3, 5056 RP Berkel-Enschot.*

MAASLAND DIZZY OX AND BOCK

Maasland is an exciting newcomer to the Dutch brewing scene. Founded in 1989 in the North Brabant region, it concentrates on organic top-fermenting beers packed with spicy hop and malt character. The brewery is strongly influenced by Belgian beers but has developed a distinctive style of its own, helped by clever marketing and eye-catching bottle labels. *D'n Schele Os* means the "Dizzy Ox" and the label shows a cross-eyed beast clearly under the influence of something stronger than milk. The 7.5 per cent abv bottle-conditioned ale is in the Low Countries style known as Tripel: it is a hazy orange-bronze colour, with a massive spicy and herbal hop aroma, rich dark grain in the mouth and a long complex finish dominated by

Opposite
The full range of the La Trappe beers, ranging from a pale Enkel to a rich and vinous Quadrupel.
Left
Organic beers from Maasland, including Dizzy Ox and an Easter Bunny beer.

spices, hops, tart fruit and malt. Much of the unusual character of the beer comes from the use of wheat and rye as well as conventional barley malt. The brewery produces three versions of a top-fermenting Bock of 6.5 per cent. Volkoren is brown in colour with a good hearty balance of dark cereal and hops; Mei (May) Bock is amber-coloured with some delicious roasted grain notes balanced by hops and dark fruit; while Het Echte Haagsche Meibock is a mouthful in every way – pale, fruity and with plenty of perfumy and peppery hops to balance the sweetness of the malt.
Maaslandbrouwerij, Kantsingel 14,
539 AJ Oss.

DE RIDDER WIECKSE WITTE

De Ridder means the Knight and this pale outrider of the Heineken empire stands on the banks of the Maas in a town that deserves to be better known for its astonishing variety of splendid bars than for a troublesome European Union treaty. De Ridder was founded in 1857 and bought by Heineken in 1982. As with Brand, the brewery is given a large amount of autonomy and brewing takes places in impressively traditional and artisanal vessels. Its major brew is a wheat beer called Wieckse Witte. *Wieckse* comes from the same root as *Wick* in Anglo-Saxon, meaning a homestead: the area of the town where the brewery stands is ancient and marked a medieval settlement by

Left
Maasland brews several versions of the Dutch style of Bock. Unlike the German versions, these are top-fermenting ales.

the river. *Witte* means white, the universal Low Countries name for a wheat beer. The 5 per cent abv beer is a blend of barley malt and wheat. While it is not spiced in the Hoegaarden fashion, both wheat and house yeast impart a spicy character to the beer, which has an aromatic hops and tart fruit aroma, a gentle, creamy grain palate and a quenching bitter-sweet finish. De Ridder also brews a Dortmunder-style amber beer with – to British visitors – the odd name of Maltezer (6.5 per cent), which means to them a chocolate drop, plus a dark, chewy and tasty Bock (7 per cent). *De Ridder Brouwerij BV, Oeverwal 3-9, 6221 EN Maastricht.*

Carlsberg

SCANDINAVIA & FINLAND

Wheat beers and sahti beers – the latter made with juniper berries as a flavouring – were the dominant styles of Scandinavia until the lager revolution of the 19th century. The work carried out at the Carlsberg breweries in Copenhagen to culture a pure strain of bottom-fermenting yeast was fundamental to the development of lager brewing. Lager beer spread like a bush fire throughout Scandinavia at a time when old rural communities and habits were being transformed by the industrial revolution and blue-collar workers were demanding more refreshing beer. The region today is dominated by large brewing groups and many lager beers tend to be thin and rather disappointing versions of the "international Pils" variety. But changing tastes and fashions and the emergence of some sturdily independent producers have seen some new and characterful lager beers emerge. The most fascinating beers of Scandinavia are the handful of porters and stouts that have survived the lager boom and which offer a glimpse of the dark beers once exported with great enthusiasm from Britain to the Baltic States, some of which clearly dropped off on their way east. Two porters are still brewed in the top-fermenting style. Surprisingly, even Carlsberg still makes a porter stout.

Opposite
An advertisement from 1935 for Carlsberg, the world famous lager from the brewery which played such a pivotal role in the development of lager brewing in the 19th century.

AASS FATØL AND BOCK

Aass – pronounced "Oss" – is Norway's oldest brewery, founded in 1834 as a simple "pot beer house", supplying customers who brought jugs to the door. It became a proper commercial concern in 1860 when Poul Lauritz Aass took control, busily expanded the business and started to export widely. The family name means summit or hill: perhaps the Aasses came from the mountains. Success was based on the quality of its interpretation of the Bavarian Bock style.

The main brand today is Fatøl, a beer so popular in Norway that it is drunk and promoted by an 8,000-strong Beer Club. Fatøl means draught beer: in bottled form it means the beer is neither filtered nor pasteurized. It is a pale lager with a spritzy palate, a malt, vanilla and hop flower aroma, and a dry, quenching finish. The 6.5 per cent abv Bock is lagered for six months and is dark, rich and creamy with a hint of fennel on the aroma and palate.

Aass produces seasonal beers and such stylistic lagers as a Münchener and a "Bayer" or Bavarian old-style dark lager – both show the influence of German brewing further north.

Aass Bryggeri, Postboks 1530, 3007 Drammen, Norway.

CARLSBERG ELEPHANT BEER AND GAMMEL PORTER IMPERIAL STOUT

Elephant Beer (7.5 per cent abv) is named after the world-famous Elephant Gate entrance to the "new" Carlsberg Brewery in the Danish capital. The original brewery stands next door and is now a fascinating museum of 19th-century brewing.

The Carlsberg enterprise was established by Jacob Christian Jacobsen, who learnt the secret of lager brewing from Sedlmayr in Munich and brought a sample of lager yeast back to Copenhagen. The first brown lagers emerged from the brewery in 1847 and 10 years later Jacobsen built a second brewery for his son. The son was called Carl and the brewery was built on a hill or berg: Carlsberg had arrived. In the Carlsberg Laboratories, the chemist Emil Christian Hansen, a disciple of Louis Pasteur, managed to isolate a pure strain of lager yeast that enabled brewers worldwide to make consistent bottom-fermenting beers. Elephant Beer is not labelled a Bock but it stands in the German style of a strong lager. It is brewed from pale malt and brewing sugar. Hallertauer hops produce 38 units of bitterness. It is a big-bodied, malty, smooth beer with delicious hints of honey sweetness balanced by the presence of tart hops. The 7.7

Opposite
Ass Fatøl is an unpasteurized and unfiltered lager beer with a cult following in Norway.

Above
Carlsberg's Elephant is a dangerously drinkable strong lager broadly in the style of German Bock beer.

per cent stout is a wonderful brewing artefact, an example of the dark beers produced in Jacobsen's original brewery. Its full name is Gammel (meaning old, from the Gammel Carlsberg Brewery) Porter Imperial Stout. It is now bottom fermenting but is a fine example of the 19th-century style, with rich dark fruit, bitter coffee and scorched vanilla notes. While Elephant is widely exported, the Porter is only available in Denmark. It deserves wider recognition.

Carlsberg Brewery, 100 Vesterfaelledvej DK 1799, Copenhagen, Denmark.

CARNEGIE PORTER

Carnegie Porter is a great survivor. In 1836 a young Scot named David Carnegie opened a brewery in Gothenburg. He was one of many Scots who looked for work in Scandinavia and the Baltic States. His brewery concentrated on dark, top-fermented ales. It was eventually merged with Sweden's biggest brewing group, Pripps. There were fears that Carnegie Porter would disappear, especially when Pripps closed the Gothenburg plant and concentrated production near Stockholm. For years it was available only as a tonic by doctor's prescription and when it reappeared in bars it was sold at a strength of 3.5 per cent abv. But now the original 5.6 per cent version has been brought back. It is superb, with a dark malt aroma reminiscent of rich Dundee cake – appropriate given the origins of the founder – a cappuccino coffee palate and a finish that becomes dry with dark malt and hops developing.

The beer is filtered and pasteurized but does improve slightly in bottle, producing a port-like note. Pripps has also introduced a vintage-dated annual version, which is matured in tanks for six months prior to bottling.

A.B.Pripps Bryggerier, Bryggeriragen 10, Stockholm-Bromma, Sweden.

Above
Carnegie Porter is a fine example of the powerful dark beers popular in Scandinavia and the Baltic countries in the last century.
Opposite
The striking Elephant Gate entrance at Carlsberg is just one of the many architectural images. The frieze shows members of the founding Jacobsen family and their workers.

Opposite
The Sinebrychoff Brewery is the oldest in Scandinavia.
Above
Koff Porter was revived for the Helsinki Olympics in 1952. Nikolai Sinebrychoff, the brewery founder, was born in a village near Moscow in 1786

KOFF PORTER

Sinebrychoff is Finland's oldest brewery, built in 1819 by a Russian, Nikolai Sinebrychoff. He brewed porter and other top-fermenting ales for the Baltic market but by 1853 he had switched to lager beer. The Finns' distrust of the Russians – frequent invaders of Finland's territory – led them to shorten the company's name to the less formidable Koff, though this causes some raised eyebrows in English-speaking countries: is it a beer or a remedy for a sore throat? Koff Porter disappeared for most of the 20th century but was brought back to commemorate the Helsinki Olympics in 1952. The brewery did not have a top-fermenting yeast and claims it cultured one from the sediment in a bottle of export Guinness: the yeast culture is still going strong. Koff Porter is 7.2 per cent abv, the strongest beer in the country. It is made from four malts and is

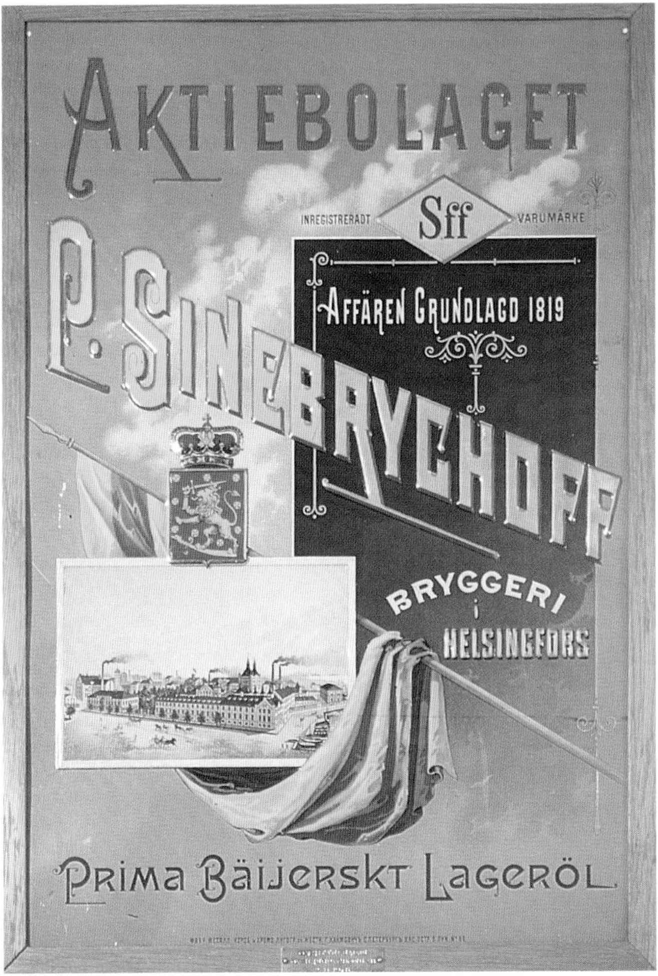

Aktiebolaget
Inregistreradt Sff Varumärke
P. Sinebrychoff
Affären Grundlagd 1819
Bryggeri
i
Helsingfors
Prima Bäijerskt Lageröl

hopped with both Northern Brewer and Hersbrücker varieties (50 units of bitterness). It is conditioned in the brewery for six weeks and is then bottled and pasteurized. The brewery, in common with Pripps, is also producing an annual vintage brew in an extremely handsome club-shaped bottle.
Aktiebolaget P. Sinebrychoff, Bryggeri i Helsingfors, Helsinki, Finland.

LAPIN KULTA

Hartwell's main address is in Helsinki but its best-known product, Lapin Kulta, is brewed in its Lapland plant, the most northerly brewery in the world. "Lapin" is removed from some export labels in case drinkers think it has some connection with rabbits, lapin being French for bunny. In fact, the only animal link with the beer are the reindeer around the brewery. The rich, rounded, malty lager is 5.3 per cent abv and is brewed from pale malt, some unmalted cereals, with Hallertauer and Saaz hops that produce 22 units of bitterness. Brewing water comes from a fjord. The beer is lagered for six months and has a smooth malty aroma, bitter-sweet malt and hops in the mouth, and some light citric fruit and hops in the finish.
Oy Hartwell AB, PO Box 31, SF-00391 Helsinki Finland.

Left
Spendrup's Old Gold is a fine example of the Pils style.
Opposite
Lapin Kulta from Lapland is brewed in the most northerly brewery in the world.

SPENDRUP OLD GOLD

Spendrup is in the suburbs of Stockholm and stands alongside a tree-fringed lake. The company is the result of several small independent breweries that combined to survive the tough clamps on alcohol by the government and the daunting size of Pripps. Spendrup has a fine traditional lager brewhouse and its Old Gold label is a premium lager of outstanding quality.

It is 5 per cent abv, has a rich malt and vanilla aroma, a quenching citric fruit palate and an intensely dry and bitter finish.

Spendrup Bryggeri AB, PO Box 6425, S-113 82 Stockholm, Sweden.

SWITZERLAND

Opposite Hürlimann's Brewery in Zurich where important work on yeast was carried out during the lager revolution.
Above Samichlaus – Santa Claus – beer is recognized as the strongest in the world and is lagered for a full year.

SAMICHLAUS

Samichlaus, at 14 per cent abv, is the world's strongest beer, listed in *The Guinness Book of Records.* The name means Santa Claus. Lagered for a full year, it is released at Christmas. The beer was made possible by the brewery's long association with the culturing of pure yeast strains. The brewery was founded in 1836 by Albert Hürlimann and the move to cold storage for lager beers demanded a more scientific knowledge of the workings of yeast. In order to produce a beer in the style of a German *doppelbock*, Hürlimann produced a yeast strain that would "not go to sleep", as brewers say, when it produced a high level of alcohol. It brewed Samichlaus as an experiment in 1979 and has made it ever since.

During fermentation, the beer is regularly roused by transferring it from one vessel to another to encourage the yeast to keep on working. The reddish-brown beer is a blend of pale and darker malts and

is hopped with Hallertauer, Hersbrücker and Styrian varieties. Units of bitterness are 30. It has a complex aroma of port wine, dried fruit, malt and peppery hops. The palate has coffee, bitter chocolate, nuts and malt while the finish is reminiscent of Rémy Martin cognac.
Brauerei Hürlimann AG, PO Box 654, 8027 Zürich.

UNITED STATES OF AMERICA

Opposite *Fritz Maytag revived Anchor Steam and created a definitive American style of beer.*

There is a brewing revolution underway in the United States. A vast country that for decades was synonymous with ice-cold, pale, over-carbonated and largely tasteless light lagers now has an abundance of choice due to the blossoming of some 800 craft or boutique breweries. The number is likely to grow to 1,000 by the turn of the century. While the craft brewers are not expected to command more than around two per cent of the total beer market they are at last offering long-suffering beer lovers an alternative to the ubiquitous Budweiser – which accounts for half the beer sold in the US – Miller Lite and Coors. In fact, the giants are sufficiently concerned by the growth of the micros that they have launched their own craft beers and bought large stockholdings in some of the bigger independents. The shape of the American beer market prior to the micro boom was the result of Prohibition in the 1920s followed by the Depression of the 1930s that combined to wipe out all but a handful of breweries: at the turn of the 20th century there were 4,000 breweries in the country, by the 1980s the number had been reduced to six nationals and 20 regionals. But then the brewing worm turned. Inspired by the pioneering work of the Campaign for Real Ale in Britain and the American Homebrewers

Association, dedicated men and women moved on from their kitchens and garages and started to brew in proper, grown-up small breweries. They refused to ape the giants. They dug deep into history books in both the US and Europe to recreate long-forgotten beer styles. They were welded to tradition. If they brewed a German Bock or Märzen, or an English India Pale Ale, porter or stout, then they made certain that such beers were true to style and to ingredients. The United States is now an exciting place in which to drink. And when you find Samuel Adams' Boston Ale, Porter, Lager and Oktoberfest on sale at St Louis airport in the home city of Budweiser you are left in no doubt that the revolutionaries have stormed the barricades.

Anchor Steam Beer

It is now part of folk lore how Fritz Maytag, an enterprising business graduate from Stanford University, bought a run-down and bankrupt brewery in San Francisco, California, in 1965 and not only transformed the face of American brewing but turned an obscure style of beer into a world-famous one. Steam Beer was a speciality spawned by the California Gold Rush

Opposite
Anchor Steam Beer is the flagship brand of the San Francisco brewery.
Above
The Anchor Brewery in the last century at the height of the California Gold Rush that created an insatiable demand for lager beer.

in the 1890s. Gold prospectors from the East Coast and the North demanded the new lager beers that were becoming fashionable there. The handful of local brewers had neither ice nor mountain caves in which to store beer. But they could get regular supplies of lager yeast.

The brewers produced a compromise, hybrid beer that was fermented at ale temperatures but using a bottom-cropping yeast in shallow fermenters that allowed the finished beer to cool quickly.

The result was a beer with such a high level of natural carbonation that when casks were tapped in San Francisco bars they were said to give off a hiss of gas that drinkers said sounded like escaping steam.

Maytag has long since moved his brewery to a state-of-the-art one complete with a German-built copper brewhouse but Steam Beer remains his main brand and he still produces it in shallow, two-feet-deep fermenters kept separate from his genuine ales. The grist is a blend of pale and crystal malts. No brewing sugars are used. Hops are Northern Brewer, added three times in the brew kettle. Following primary fermentation, the beer is warm conditioned for three weeks and then *kräusened* with some partially-fermented wort to start a second fermentation. The 5 per cent abv beer is bronze-coloured and highly complex, with a malty-nutty aroma, malt and light fruit in the mouth and a finish in which the hops slowly dominate. It has 30 to 35 units of bitterness. It is clean and quenching like a lager but also has a decidedly ale-like fruitiness. Anchor's ales include Liberty Ale, bursting with American hop character, Porter, Wheat Beer and Old Foghorn barley wine.

Anchor Brewing Company, 1705 Mariposa Street, San Francisco, California 94107.

BOSTON ALE AND LAGER

Jim Koch (pronounced Cook) is a descendant of Bavarian brewers who brought their skills to the US but were forced out of business during a spate of mergers in the 1950s. Koch gave up a career in 1985 to brew and sell beer. Now one of the biggest independent craft brewers, his

Above
Charles Jerome, (second left) in 1906, was the great-great-grandfather of Jim Koch, founder of the Boston Brewery.
Right
Louis Koch's Brewery in St Louis, in 1870, was the birthplace of the original recipe for Boston Lager.

Above
Samuel Adams, the brewer who organized the Boston Tea Party, adorns the beers from the Boston Brewery.

beers are contract brewed in several states as well as in Boston. His beers carry the name of Samuel Adams – as well as being one of the key figures in the American revolution, Adams was also a professional brewer. Koch's first beer was Samuel Adams Boston Lager (4.4 per cent abv), a golden, rounded, firm-bodied lager in the Munich style, brewed from pale and Munich malts and hopped with Hallertauer Mittlefrüh. It has a floral hop aroma, malty palate and a big, malty-hoppy finish.

Samuel Adams Boston Ale (5 per cent) restores the old New England style known as "Stock Ale", a well-matured beer that was used for blending with younger ales. Boston Ale is made from pale and crystal malts and is hopped three times in the brew kettle with English Fuggles and Czech Saaz and then dosed with Kent Goldings during maturation. It is *kräusened* and cold conditioned, has a burnished amber colour, a big peppery hop aroma, a tart and fruity palate and a big malt, hops, fruit and cobnuts finish.

Boston Brewing also produces a Cream Stout, a Honey Porter and a Triple Bock that at 17.5 per cent seems set to knock Samichlaus of Switzerland off its "world's strongest beer" perch.

Boston Beer Company, 30 Germania Street, Boston, Massachussets 02130.

Brooklyn Lager, Brown Ale and Chocolate Stout

Brooklyn, one of the celebrated New York City boroughs, lost both its baseball team – the Dodgers – and its 40 breweries. The decline of a brewing tradition dating from the Dutch colonists of the "broken line" suburb was the result of Prohibition, Depression and 1950s mergers and closures.

The tradition was revived in the 1980s by journalist and home-brewer Steve Hindy and banker Tom Potter. They were advised by veteran brewer Bill Moeller, who was keen to recreate a pre-Prohibition lager. Brooklyn Lager (5.5 per cent abv) is an indication of how rich and full-bodied American lagers must have been before the Charge of the Lite Brigade. It is almost ale-like in character. It is brewed from crystal as well as pale malt and is dry hopped. It has a rich malt, hops and cobnuts aroma, there is ripe malt in the mouth and has a long finish full of malt and hops character. Brooklyn Brown is a top fermenting ale (6 per cent) made from pale, crystal, chocolate and black malts and hopped with Cascade and Northern Brewer. It is dry hopped, with a chocolate and coffee aroma and palate, and a dry, nutty and hoppy finish.

Opposite *Brooklyn Lager recreates the style of beer destroyed by Prohibition, the Depression and merger mania.*
Opposite Right *Brooklyn now has a range of occasional beers, including a full-bodied and chocolatey stout.*

When Garrett Oliver, former brewmaster at the Manhattan Brewery, moved over the bridge to join Brooklyn, he added a winter Black Chocolate Stout to the range (8.3 per cent) that

became a cult beer almost overnight throughout New York City. It is brewed from pale and dark malts, has a big burnt roasted malt, bitter chocolate, dark fruit and hops aroma and palate and is a contender for Imperial Stout status. Oliver has also brewed a dry India Pale Ale with a pronounced citric note. The Brooklyn beers were originally contracted brewed but its own plant was opened in 1996.

Brooklyn Brewery, 79 North 11th Street, Brooklyn, New York 11211.

Above
Geary of Portland, Maine, has an acclaimed Pale Ale and an occasional London-style Porter.
Opposite
Bert Grant's Brewery is based in the hop fields of Yakima in Washington State.

GEARY PALE ALE

David Geary learnt his brewing skills in England and Scotland – he trained at Traquair House – which helps explain the exceptional quality of his Pale Ale. His brewing equipment was installed by Peter Austin, known as the "father" of the British micro-brewing revolution who has now installed his craft brewhouses in the US, France and even China.

When David Geary and his wife Karen launched their brewery in the mid-1980s there was just a handful of kindred spirits on the East Coast. David Geary's Pale Ale encouraged others to follow in his footsteps. He imports two-row English pale, crystal and chocolate malts from England and uses Cascade and Mount Hood hops from the Pacific North-west, Tettnanger from Germany and English

Fuggles. The 4.5 per cent abv ale has a massive floral and citric hop aroma and palate with a restrained fruitiness in the finish. Geary also brews a winter Hampshire Special Ale, with a label showing boats frozen in the Maine, and a big spicy hop character, plus a roasty, hoppy, liquorice London Porter.
D.L. Geary Brewing Company, 38 Evergreen Drive, Portland, Maine 04103.

GRANT'S SCOTTISH ALE.

Bert Grant's brewery is in the heart of the Pacific North-west's hop country, on the eastern side of the Cascade Mountains where the warm, dry climate imparts a powerful citric fruit character to such local varieties as the one named after the surrounding mountain range. Grant has three passports: he was born in Scotland, grew up in Canada where he worked as a chemist for Canadian Breweries, and migrated across the border to work for Stroh in Detroit before moving to Yakima to build a hop-processing plant.

His home-brewing efforts were applauded and he decided to go full-time. He started in the old Yakima Opera House and eventually moved to a greenfield site on the edge of town. He also has a separate brew-pub next to the redundant Yakima railroad station. Grant is not a shrinking violet: he calls his Scottish Ale "the best beer in the world". The beer is 5.6 per cent abv. Grant uses a generous amount of crystal

Opposite *Mendocino's Red Tail Ale and Black Hawk Stout, like all of the brewery's beers, are named after Californian birds.*

malt alongside pale, giving the beer an amber colour and a nutty roastiness in the mouth. The hoppiness (45 units of bitterness) comes from Cascades in the brew kettle and Willamettes, an American Fuggle derivative, for dry hopping. The beer has a rich sultana fruitiness balanced by pungent hops on the aroma, and a dry and fruity finish. Grant also brews a Celtic Ale, an intensely hoppy IPA, a chocolatey Porter and an Imperial Stout with a resounding 100 units of bitterness.

Grant's Yakima Brewing & Malting Company, 1803 Presson Place, Yakima, Washington 98902

Mendocino Red Tail Ale and Black Hawk Stout

Mendocino has the address that other craft brewers would kill for: Hopland, some 90 miles north of San Francisco. It is based in an old saloon in Mendocino County and was founded by Michael Laybourn, Norman Franks and John Scahill in 1982, who planted hops amid the grape vines.

It was California's first brewpub since Prohibition and the hops were the first to be grown in the region since the early 1950s, when the industry moved north to the cooler climes of Oregon and Washington.

All the beers are named after birds. Red Tail (5.5 per cent abv) is brewed from pale and crystal malts and hopped with Cascade and Cluster varieties. It has a superb citric hop

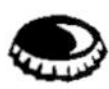

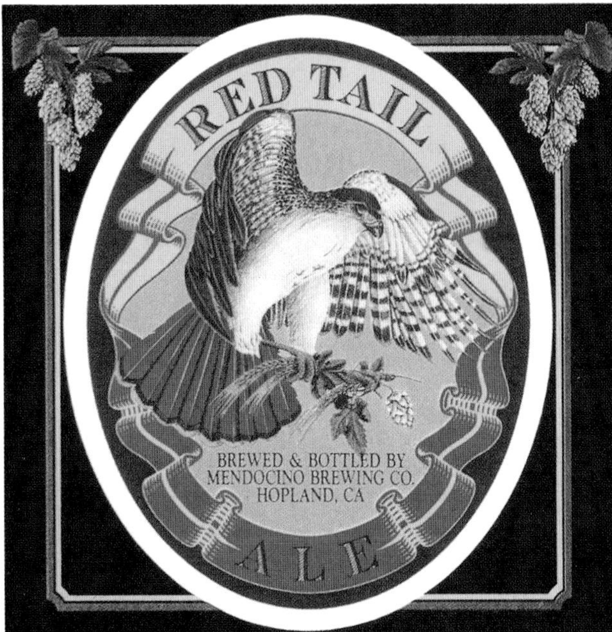

RED TAIL
BREWED & BOTTLED BY
MENDOCINO BREWING CO.
HOPLAND, CA
ALE

GOVERNMENT WARNING: (1) ACCORDING TO THE SURGEON GENERAL, WOMEN SHOULD NOT DRINK ALCOHOLIC BEVERAGES DURING PREGNANCY BECAUSE OF THE RISK OF BIRTH DEFECTS. (2) CONSUMPTION OF ALCOHOLIC BEVERAGES IMPAIRS YOUR ABILITY TO DRIVE A CAR OR OPERATE MACHINERY, AND MAY CAUSE HEALTH PROBLEMS.
Brewed And Bottled By
MENDOCINO
BREWING
COMPANY
EST.
1982
BLACK HAWK
STOUT
HOPLAND, CALIFORNIA
SPECIAL
EDITION
CA CASH REFUND
1 PINT 6 FL OZ

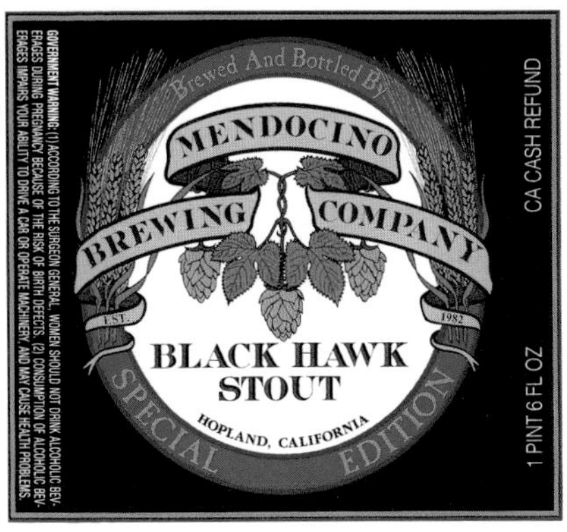

Opposite *Pete Slosberg's fogeyish "Wicked" labels have turned him into one of the biggest of the American craft brewers. As well as his flagship Wicked Ale, he now produces a wide range of beers, including a fruity and creamy Honey Wheat.*

aroma with rounded malt in the mouth and a long finish balanced between malt, hops and citric fruit.

Black Hawk Stout (5.8 per cent abv) is a classic, packed with dark malt, coffee, bitter chocolate and fruit with a good underpinning of hops and a residual sweetness in the finish that means this is not another attempt at a dry Irish stout but a genuine American version. It is as smooth and dangerously drinkable as a chocolate liqueur. The company also brews Peregrine Pale Ale and Heron Pale Ale.

Mendocino Brewing Company, 13551 South Highway 101, Hopland, California 95449.

Pete's Wicked Ale

Pete Slosberg is one of America's major craft brewers, even though all his beers are contract brewed for him. He is a former marketing man in California's Silicon Valley who turned his home-brewing hobby into a commercial enterprise. When his Palo Alto brewery failed he moved brewing to other companies. His Wicked Ale is now made in St Paul, Minnesota. Originally top fermenting, it is now made by bottom fermentation – a wicked rewriting of the rules. It is, nevertheless, a remarkable beer, honoured many times with awards at the Great American Beer Festival.

At 5 per cent abv, it is brewed from pale, crystal and black malts and hopped with Cascades. It has a deep bronze colour with a

distinctive chocolate and slightly vinous palate. Slosberg's rapidly-expanding range includes a Lager and a superb Honey Wheat Beer plus seasonal specialities.

Pete's Brewing Company, 514 High Street, Palo Alto, California 94301.

Pike Place Pale Ale and East India Pale Ale

Pike Place is in Seattle's smart harbourside market and restaurant area. The brewery was founded in 1989 by Charles Finkel, who also runs an importing business called Merchant du Vin. In spite of the name, Finkel is a major importer of European beers and has turned Samuel Smith of England into a major player in the US. The tiny brewery is wedded to tradition. The two pales ales are based on authentic English recipes and Finkel spares no effort or money in importing floor-malted

Above
The tiny Pike Place Brewery in Seattle's Harbour area brews a Pale Ale and an East India variant that boom with malt and hop character.

Maris Otter barley from Norfolk along with crystal malt and East Kent Goldings. Pale Ale (5.5 per cent abv) has an astounding 20 per cent crystal malt in its make-up, giving it a deep amber colour, with a peppery hop aroma, a biscuity palate, and hops and dark fruit in the finish. East India Pale Ale (7 per cent) is brewed with pale, carapils and Munich malts and is hopped with Chinook and British Columbia varieties as well as Goldings. It is tawny-gold in colour, has a massive grapefruit aroma from the Chinooks, more tart fruit in the mouth and a powerful hoppy finish. Pike Place also has a

Left
Pyramid of Seattle's beers are based on original recipes, though perhaps not as ancient as the time of the Pharoahs.

smooth and chocolatey Porter. Its Old Bawdy barley wine commemorates the fact that the brewery stands on the site of a former brothel. *Pike Place Brewery, 1432 Western Avenue, Seattle, Washington 98101.*

PYRAMID HEFEWEIZEN

Pyramid is one of the many energetic, fast-growing and adventurous craft breweries in the Pacific North-west. It brews ales under the Pyramid name with lagers branded as Thomas Kemper. As well as the original brewery in the old logging town of Kalama it now has a second plant in Seattle and opened a third in San Francisco in January 1977. Its ales and lagers have won a series of awards at the Great American Beer Festival and other American

brewing events for beers firmly based on authentic European styles and recipes. Its Hefeweizen (5.1 per cent abv) is an unfiltered, bottle-conditioned Bavarian wheat beer, brewed from two-row pale barley malt, wheat and caramel with Nugget and Perle hops. It has a spicy and fruity aroma, with smooth and

creamy grain in the mouth and a long, refreshing finish with powerful hints of apple fruit and spices.

Among its burgeoning range of ales and lagers, its Thomas Kemper Bohemian Dunkel won a bronze prize for dark lagers at the 1996 Great American Festival in Denver. Other beers include an English-style Pale Ale, an Apricot fruit beer, a Porter and an Espresso Stout.
Pyramid Ales Brewery, 110 W. Marine Drive, Kalama, Washington 98625.

Redhook ESB

Redhook is the biggest new-wave brewery in the North-west. It started in a converted trolley barn in down-town Seattle, built a second greenfield brewery on the edge of town and is now planning a third plant on the East Coast in Portsmouth, New Hampshire. The expansion has been the result of a deal with Anheuser-Busch, the Budweiser giant, which markets Redhook beers nationally in return for a substantial 25 per cent stake in the independent. It remains to be seen whether Redhook has entered into a Faustian pact. The company's dedication to quality cannot be gainsayed. ESB stands for Extra Special Bitter and the inspiration comes clearly from the magnificent draught English pale ale of the same name brewed in London by Fullers.

Above
Redhook's wide range of beers includes a rich and fruity interpretation of the Extra Special Bitter style.

Redhook's version is the stand-out beer of the range: 5.4 per cent abv, it has a pronounced orange fruitiness like its English counterpart. It is brewed from pale and crystal malts, Willamette and Tettnanger hops and an English top-fermenting yeast strain. Rich citric fruit and ripe, slightly toasty malt dominate aroma and palate, with a long dry, quenching finish with a spicy hop note and tangy fruit. Other Redhook products include a Rye Beer, a Blackhook Porter and a Wheat Hook. Let's hope the company doesn't get a Right Hook from Anheuser-Busch.

Redhook Brewery, 3400 Phinney Avenue North, Seattle, Washington 98103.

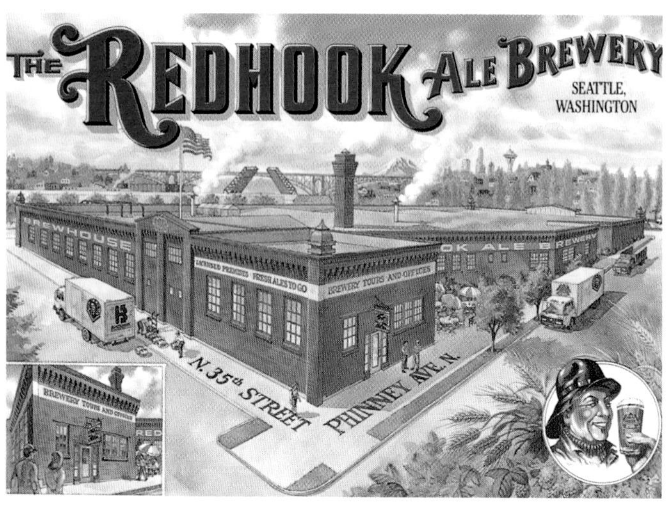

Opposite
Redhook's first brewery was based in a former trolley station (tram garage) in the Swedish area of Seattle.
Left
A brilliant barley wine and one of the strongest beers brewed in the US.

Sierra Nevada Big Foot Barley Wine

Sierra Nevada in Chico, northern California, was one of the first craft breweries, founded in 1981 by Ken Grossman and Paul Camusi. Its bottle-conditioned Big Foot is a world classic barley wine and at 12.5 per cent abv is one of the strongest beers brewed in the US. It has a big aroma of earthy hops and dark malt, massive warming alcohol in the mouth and finish bursting with dark fruit and spicy hops. The hops are Nugget for bitterness, with an addition of Cascades and Centennial for aroma during conditioning. The beer is conditioned in the brewery for four weeks then released. It will remain in good condition for two years, developing a profound vinous note. Sierra Nevada also produces a Lager, Pale Ale, Porter and Stout.

Sierra Nevada Brewing Company, 1075 East 20th Street, Chico, California 95928.

Canada

Opposite
Unibroue's End of the World beer is a big, fruity and spicy ale while Blanche de Chambly is inspired by Belgian "white" beers.

Canada is understandably influenced by events in its neighbour's country to the south. It had an even longer period of Prohibition than the United States – from the start of World War One to 1932. And with a similar result: the brewing industry was reduced to a handful of giants that had managed to survive the long close-down. Their domination was intensified by severe restrictions on the retailing of beer. It cannot, for example, be carried across the border from one province to another, a policy that favours big companies able to build breweries in each province. The big three began as ale brewers but switched to the production of light and undemanding lagers.

In 1989 two of the brewing giants, Carling and Molson, merged, giving the new group half the beer market. Labatt, the other giant, bought Rolling Rock in the US and then in 1995 became part of the Belgian Interbrew group, now a world mega-brewing corporation. While Labatt and Molson concentrate on such cold and sticky products as "ice beer", characterful products are beginning to emerge from a new wave of micros, including several in the French-speaking areas: many of the original French settlers came from northern France and brought with them a brewing tradition rather than a wine one. Many of their products can only be drunk on draught but some are now expanding into bottle production as well.

UNIBROUE BLANCHE DE CHAMBLY AND LA FIN DU MONDE

Unibroue, in a suburb of Montreal, specializes in bottle-conditioned beers. It was founded in 1990 by two admirers of Belgian ales, André Dion and the rock singer Robert Charlebois. Head brewer Gino Vantieghem comes from Belgium, which adds to the authenticity of the beers he brews. Blanche de Chambly (5 per cent abv) is firmly in the Belgian style of "white" wheat beer, with a spicy aroma, citric fruit in the mouth and a long, dry finish balanced between tart fruit and spices. La Fin

Opposite *Upper Canada's beers recall the days of the pioneers with a malty lager and an earthy, peppery, English-style ale.*

du Monde (9 per cent) means "the End of the World" and vies with Belgium's Morte Subite ("Sudden Death") as the most forbidding beer name in the world. But Unibroue insists the beer has no hidden terrors and the name merely implies you would have to travel to the ends of the earth to find a better drink. It is the Grand Cru to the Blanche: a big, golden ale that throws a massive head, with citric fruit and spices on the aroma and palate, and a long, vinous and hoppy finish. Unibroue also produces an 8 per cent Mudite, Raftman (5.5 per cent) brewed with whisky malt and La Gaillarde, based on medieval recipes and brewed with herbs and spices in place of hops. All these remarkable beers are aided by some brilliantly imaginative labels.
Unibroue, 80 rue Carrières, Chambly, Quebec J3L 2H6.

Upper Canada Dark Ale, Rebellion Ale and Rebellion Lager

Upper Canada uses the early settlers' name for the province of Ontario. The brewery was founded in 1985 by Frank Heaps who is proud to claim on his labels that his beers are "free from adjuncts, additives and chemicals". They are also unpasteurized. Dark Ale (5 per cent abv), has crystal, a paler carastan and black malt blended with pale. Hops are two American varieties, Cascade and Cluster. This amber-

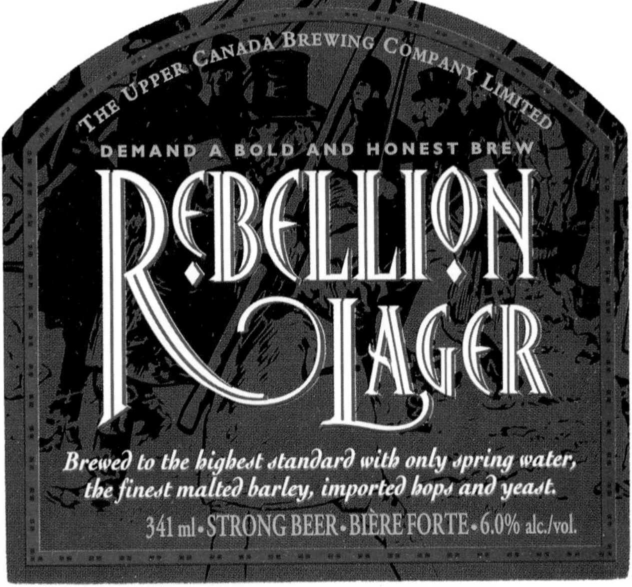
THE UPPER CANADA BREWING COMPANY LIMITED
DEMAND A BOLD AND HONEST BREW
REBELLION LAGER
Brewed to the highest standard with only spring water, the finest malted barley, imported hops and yeast.
341 ml • STRONG BEER • BIÈRE FORTE • 6.0% alc./vol.

THE UPPER CANADA BREWING COMPANY LIMITED
DEMAND A BOLD AND HONEST BREW
REBELLION ALE
Brewed to the highest standard with only spring water, the finest malted barley, imported hops and yeast.
341 ml • ALE • 5.2% alc./vol.

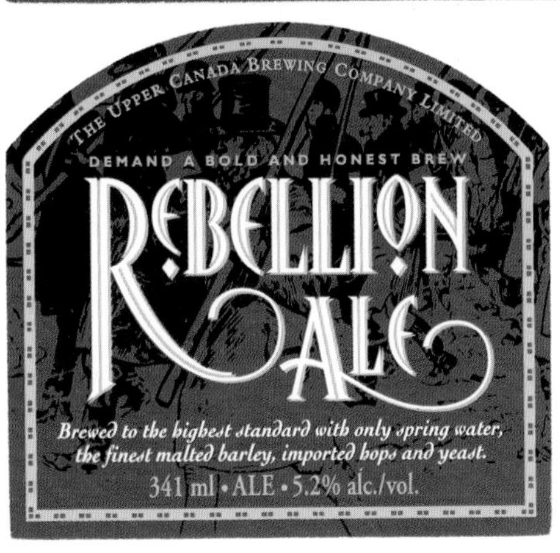

Opposite *Wellington has a dual inspiration: the Iron Duke and the English family brewery of Arkell. It brews an English-style bitter ale and a porter named in honour of the man who defeated Bonaparte.*

coloured ale has a fruity, yeasty and malty aroma, with citric fruit from the hops in the mouth and a malty finish balanced by good hop bitterness. Rebellion Ale (5.2 per cent) is brewed from pale and carastan malts and hopped only with English Challenger. It is brewed in the English pale ale style and has a powerful earthy, peppery aroma from the hops, with tart fruit and hops in the mouth, and a long, lingering finish dominated by hop bitterness and citric fruit. Rebellion Lager (6 per cent) has just pale malt with Northern Brewer as the main hop and two late additions of Hersbrücker. It has a malt and vanilla aroma with perfumy hops, a firm malty body and a rich malt and hops finish. The head brewer, Richard Rench, is originally from Britain and learnt his craft with the great brewers of Burton on Trent. He also brews a stout, a wheat beer and a Bock.

Upper Canada Brewing Company, 2 Atlantic Avenue, Toronto, Ontario M6K 1X8.

Wellington Arkell Best Bitter

Arkell is a well-known family brewery in Swindon, southern England and it is odd to find its name cropping up on a beer in Canada. The link is through a member of the English Arkell family who founded a community in Guelph, 40 miles from Toronto, once an important brewing centre, with a fine supply of hard spring water that is ideal for brewing pale ales. Arkell Best Bitter (4 per cent), available in cask-conditioned form as well as in bottle, has a peppery aroma from English Kent Goldings hops, tart citric fruit and juicy malt in the mouth and long hoppy-fruity finish. As a result of the Wellington connection, the brewery makes an Iron Duke Ale (6.5 per cent) and Iron Duke Porter (5.7 per cent), as well as a rich and malty County Ale (5 per cent) and a Premium Lager (4.5 per cent).

Wellington County Brewery, 950 Woodlawn Road West, Guelph, Ontario N1K 1B8.

Latin America

Opposite
Brahma shows how well Pilsner travelled from Central Europe to Latin America.

Latin American beer is about more than thin lagers drunk straight from the bottle with wedges of lime stuck in the necks. Corona and Sol, briefly cult drinks among modish but fickle young drinkers in San Francisco, New York and London, have tended to mask the long and rich traditions of brewing in the vast continent. Long before Europeans arrived in Latin America natives were making beers from fermented corn stalks and maize while a black beer was brewed in the Upper Amazon from at least the 15th century. The Europeans brought with them the lager tradition. This influence was greatest in Mexico, which was briefly an Austrian colony and learnt from the Austrians the art of making the Vienna Red style of amber lager perfected by Anton Dreher. The Germans were also busily at work in Latin America and the continent today is dominated by pale lagers, ranging from extremely thin and uninspired interpretations of the style to some notably characterful ones, particularly in Brazil.

Brahma Lager

Brazil was invaded by the Portuguese rather than the Spanish but the modern brewing tradition is Germanic. Brahma (5 per cent abv) is a remarkably fine example of an amber-to-gold lager with a rich malt and cornflour aroma, a firm malty palate and a bitter-sweet finish with a late burst of hops. Aficionados

may care to argue whether it is in the Pilsen, Munich or Dortmund styles. Most remarkably, the company, which produces 31 million hectolitres a year, also brews a top-fermenting, 8 per cent abv porter, testimony to the worldwide impact of the London style prior to the lager revolution. To "porter sniffers", endlessly arguing about the origins of the name, comes another pedantic twist: porter is named not after London market workers but Portugal!

Cia. Cervejaria Brahma, Filial Rio, Rua Marqués de Sapucai, 20215-900 Rio de Janeiro, Brazil.

Dos Equis

Moctezuma dates from 1894 and today is the biggest brewery in Mexico since its merger with the Cuauhtémoc group. The group is best known for Sol, the extraordinarily ordinary lager in a clear glass bottle that helped spawn the worldwide craze for lager-and-lime. Of far greater interest is Dos Equis (4.8 per cent abv), an amber lager brewed broadly in the Vienna style, with a rich dark fruit and chocolate aroma and palate and some light hop notes in the finish. The name means Two Crosses, from the ancient European tradition of blessing beer by marking crosses on casks. Moctezuma and

DOS EQUIS
XX
IMPORTED BEER
PRODUCT OF MEXICO
33 cl
DOS EQUIS
XX
SPECIAL LAGER
DOS EQUIS
XX
IMPORTED BEER
PRODUCT OF MEXICO
DOS EQUIS
XX
BEER·BIER·BIRRA·BIERE
CERVEZA
33 cl

Cuauhtémoc also brew a good Pils-type lager called Bohemia and a less distinctive refresher called Carta Blanca, once promoted as "the Gulp of Mexico".

Cervecerìa Moctezuma, Avenido Alfonso Reyes 2202, Nte, Monterrey NL 64442, Mexico.

NEGRA MODELO

Modelo has Mexico's biggest brewing plant in the capital city. It brews a vast range of beers, including its competitor to Sol, Corona. Negra Modelo (5.3 per cent abv, with 19 units of bitterness) is dark brown rather than black and is halfway between a Vienna Red and a Munich Dunkel. It has a strong chocolatey aroma and palate from the use of well-cured dark malt, and a long finish with a hint of spice, more chocolate, delicate hops and a dry roastiness.

Cervecarìa Modelo, 156 Lago Alberto, Mexico City 11320.

Opposite
Dos Equis – Two Crosses – is a Mexican beer inspired by the Vienna Red style.

PERU GOLD

Peru's leading beer carries a label of a native face mask. The impressive lager is 5 per cent abv and has a rich corn and vanilla aroma, is tart and malty in the mouth, and has a dry and quenching finish with some citric fruit from the hops. The company also makes Cuzco Peruvian Beer.

Cia. Cervecera del Sur del Perü, SA, Fábica Dorada, Variante de Uchumayo 1801, Casilla 43, Arequipa, Peru.

Africa

Opposite & below Mauritius has won many prizes for its beers, including Blue Marlin lager.

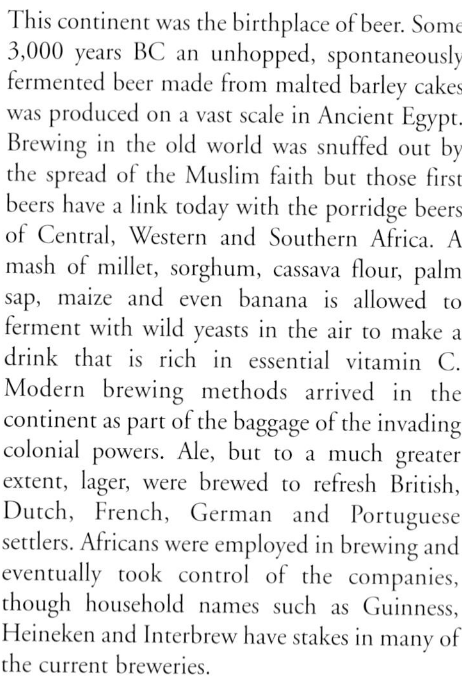

This continent was the birthplace of beer. Some 3,000 years BC an unhopped, spontaneously fermented beer made from malted barley cakes was produced on a vast scale in Ancient Egypt. Brewing in the old world was snuffed out by the spread of the Muslim faith but those first beers have a link today with the porridge beers of Central, Western and Southern Africa. A mash of millet, sorghum, cassava flour, palm sap, maize and even banana is allowed to ferment with wild yeasts in the air to make a drink that is rich in essential vitamin C. Modern brewing methods arrived in the continent as part of the baggage of the invading colonial powers. Ale, but to a much greater extent, lager, were brewed to refresh British, Dutch, French, German and Portuguese settlers. Africans were employed in brewing and eventually took control of the companies, though household names such as Guinness, Heineken and Interbrew have stakes in many of the current breweries.

Blue Marlin and Phoenix

For a small island, Mauritius has had impressive success with the lager beers produced by its brewery. Blue Marlin (5.6 per cent abv) was introduced in 1989 and won a gold medal in the Monde Sélection competition three years later. Phoenix (4.5 per cent) won a gold at the International Brewers Exhibition (Brewex) in

1983 and a gold at Monde Sélection in 1989. Blue Marlin has a good hop aroma with rich toffee and malt in the mouth and a long finish with some citric fruit notes. Phoenix is a fine refreshing beer with delicate hop and malt on the nose, a light malty body and a spritzy finish with a late burst of hop bitterness.
Mauritius Brewery, Phoenix, Mauritius.

Opposite
Tusker Lager – famed as one of Ernest Hemingway's favourite tipples.
Above
Guinness Foreign Extra is a cult drink in Africa and is claimed to have remarkable powers.

NIGERIAN GUINNESS

Guinness has three breweries in Nigeria, where their stout is a cult drink. The Anglo-Irish brewing group has plants in several other African countries, where stout is widely considered an aphrodisiac. Guinness frowns on such unofficial promotions as "a baby in every bottle" and "it puts lead in your pencil". Nigerian and several other African versions of Guinness are based on Foreign Extra Stout (see Irish section) but are fractionally higher in alcohol at 8 per cent abv.

The Nigerian plants make a conventional pale beer that is blended with hopped wort made in Dublin. The wort is boiled and evaporated and turned into a syrup similar to home-brewers' malt extract and sent to Nigeria. The finished blend lacks the lactic sourness of FES but it has a rich and rounded roasted barley, dark fruit and bitter hops aroma and palate and, for such a strong beer, a surprisingly delicate, bitter finish.

c/o Arthur Guinness & Son, St James's Gate, Dublin 8, Ireland.

TUSKER PREMIUM LAGER

One of the most characterful Pilsner-style beers in Africa comes from a brewery founded by British settlers, including a gold prospector. East African Breweries, as it was first called, imported both equipment and a brewer from

Britain: the brewer came from the famous brewing town of Burtonwood near Warrington in North-west England. Hops were imported from Kent and the main products were ale and stout.

Lager brewing was developed in the 1930s and the brewery's two main products were boosted by the frequent presence of Ernest Hemingway on big game hunts in Kenya, who said that White Cap and Tusker were his favourite beers. Tusker Premium (4.8 per cent abv) is brewed from 90 per cent pale barley malt and 10 per cent cane sugar and is hopped with imported Hallertauer and Styrian hops. It has a fine Pilsner-style aroma of malt, vanilla and perfumy hops, with malt and hops balanced in the mouth and a long, delicate malty finish that becomes dry and hoppy.

The beer's name comes from an incident when one of the founders of the brewery was unfortunately killed by an elephant: it seems rather harsh that the killer, not the victim, gets the glory on the label.

Kenya Brewery, Thika Road, Ruaraka, Nairobi, Kenya.

SAPPORO EXPORT BEER
ASAHI BEER
ASAHI
LAGER-BEER
DAI NIPPON BREWERY COMPANY LIMITED TOKYO JAPAN
YEBISU BEER
YEBISU
LAGER-BEER
DAI NIPPON BREWERY COMPANY LIMITED TOKYO JAPAN
SAPPOROBEER
SAPPORO
LAGER-BEER
DAI NIPPON BREWERY COMPANY LIMITED TOKYO JAPAN
NIPPON BREWERY Co. Ltd.
TOKYO. OSAKA.

ASIA & THE FAR EAST

Brewing is a recent arrival in Japan. Alcohol made from rice has a centuries-old tradition but beer was unknown until an American trade mission brought some supplies of beer with it in 1853 and the fascinated Japanese hurried to learn the skills of brewing. An American company, Wiegand and Copeland, built a brewery in Yokohama that eventually became the locally-owned Kirin. But most of the modern breweries were built by Germans, which explains why the big four producers, Asahi, Kirin, Sapporo and Suntory, now concentrate on pale lagers. Interesting sidelines include black lagers that reflect the German styles of Franconia and Thuringia, plus some stouts that stem from Britain's presence here in the last century. China is set to become one of the world's major brewing nations. Many international brewing giants have recently moved into China, building links with existing breweries. Only one long-standing company exports on a regular basis, but it is likely that once the internal market is satisfied many more Chinese breweries, under Western tutelage, will look for additional sales. Singapore has a famous lager beer, India, with its links to Britain, continues to make a few stouts and lagers — but sadly no India Pale Ales — while a world-class stout can be found in Sri Lanka.

Opposite
An old Sapporo advertisement with a geisha lending an air of refinement to the brewery's wares.

China

Tsingtao Lager

When the Germans leased the port of Tsingtao on the Shantung peninsula close to Japan and Korea they naturally built a brewery that survives and thrives. The name of the port is now spelt Qingdao but the old name is used on the labels of the extremely pale Pilsner-style lager that is exported to 30 countries. The American Budweiser giant Anheuser-Busch has a small 5 per cent shareholding: the beer has a cult following in the US among aficionados of Chinese cooking. China now has its own barley and hop varieties though supplies and quality are erratic. The 5.2 per cent abv beer, when it is on form, has a good Pilsner malt and hop attack with some vanilla notes in the finish.

Qingdao Brewery, 56 Dengzhou Road, Qingdao, Shandong 266021.

Japan

Asahi Stout

The 8 per cent abv Stout is one of the most fascinating beers brewed in the Japanese islands. It is a true top-fermenting beer that, remarkably, uses a wild Brettanomyces yeast culture during fermentation that gives it a slightly sour and lactic note. It has a big and powerful palate laced with dark fruit and hops, a dry and pungent aroma and a long, soft, vinous finish with hints of rich, dark cake. Here, across the world from London, is a proud

Opposite
Tsingtao – China's only widely exported beer.
Left
Asahi Stout, Kirin Stout and Lager – classics from a country with a relatively short brewing history, that holds beer in increasingly high regard.

and honourable member of the Imperial Stout style, perfected in the English capital in the 19th century for export to the Baltic States. Asahi also makes one of the German-inspired Black Beers: it is 5 per cent abv, reddish-brown rather than black with a sweet malt and caramel aroma and palate.
Asahi Breweries, 23-1 Azumabashi 1-chome, Sumida-ku, Tokyo 130.

KIRIN LAGER AND STOUT

Named after a mythical creature that is half dragon and half horse, Kirin makes the most distinctive of Japan's Pilsner-style lagers. It is 4.9 per cent abv with 27 units of bitterness and is lagered for an impressive two months. It is hopped with Hallertauer and Saaz varieties. It has a rich malty aroma with a good balance of malt, honey and hops in the mouth and a long,

キリンビール
KIRIN BREWERY CO

dry and hoppy finish. Kirin Stout is 8 per cent and is now bottom fermenting, bitter-sweet, with dark toffee notes.
Kirin Brewery Company, 26-1, Jingumae 6-chome, Shibuya-ko, Tokyo 150.

Opposite
An old advertisement for Kirin Lager, the brand leader from Japan's brewing giant.
Below
Yebisu is named after a Shinto god.

Sapporo Black Beer and Yebisu

The most impressive is Yebisu, named after a Shinto god. It is a fragrant, firm-bodied malty beer in the Dortmunder Export style, with a good underpinning of hops from the use of Hallertauer Mittelfrüh and Hersbrücker varieties. The beer is 5 per cent abv with a rich burnished gold colour. Sapporo's Black Beer is also 5 per cent, brewed from a combination of pale, crystal, Munich and crystal malts and a small amount of rice. It has 25 bitterness units from home-grown and imported hops. It has a deep, opaque colour with a ruby tinge, a roasted coffee aroma, a palate reminiscent of dark, rich fruit, and a malty finish with toffee notes and bitter hops.
Sapporo Breweries, 7-10-1 Ginza, Chuo-ku, Tokyo 104.

INDIA

KINGFISHER LAGER

Kingfisher has become a major international lager brand. It is especially popular in Britain, where it is brewed under licence by Shepherd Neame of Kent, and is available in many Asian restaurants. The 5 per cent abv beer is burnished gold and is more in the Dortmunder than the Pilsner tradition, with a juicy malt aroma, a toasty palate and a balance of malt and hops in the finish.

Premier Breweries, Kanjikode West PO 678, Palghat, Kerala.

SINGAPORE

TIGER BEER

Above
"Time for a Tiger" – the beer's slogan was immortalized by Anthony Burgess.

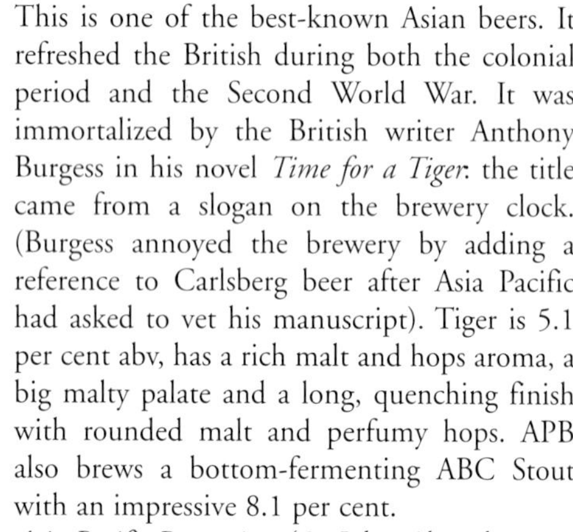

This is one of the best-known Asian beers. It refreshed the British during both the colonial period and the Second World War. It was immortalized by the British writer Anthony Burgess in his novel *Time for a Tiger*: the title came from a slogan on the brewery clock. (Burgess annoyed the brewery by adding a reference to Carlsberg beer after Asia Pacific had asked to vet his manuscript). Tiger is 5.1 per cent abv, has a rich malt and hops aroma, a big malty palate and a long, quenching finish with rounded malt and perfumy hops. APB also brews a bottom-fermenting ABC Stout with an impressive 8.1 per cent.

Asia Pacific Breweries, 459 Jalan Ahmad Ibrahim, Singapore 9111.

SRI LANKA

LION STOUT

One of the world's finest top-fermenting stouts comes from the Ceylon Brewery in the tea-planting region of Sri Lanka, close to the Buddhist Holy City of Kandy. The brewery was built in the late 19th century to refresh British tea-planters and it has a plentiful supply of pure brewing liquor from the nearby Lovers' Leap Waterfall. The 7.5 per cent abv, bottle-conditioned beer is brewed from British, Czech and Danish malts with Styrian hops and an English yeast strain. All the ingredients are transported along precarious roads to the brewery located 3,500 feet above sea level.

The luscious stout has a big espresso coffee and bitter chocolate aroma and palate with some vinous fruit and bitter hops in the finish. The beer is sold in cask-conditioned form in a couple of outlets near the brewery. In Colombo, McCallum's Three Coins Brewery also brews a Sando Stout: this is bottom fermenting and, in common with Murphy's in faraway Cork, Ireland, once used the Hungarian strongman Sando to promote the beer.

Ceylon Brewery, Nuwara Eliya, Kandy, Sri Lanka.

Australia

Opposite
Cascade of Tasmania is the oldest working brewery in Australia, producing some of the best lagers in the country.

The early settlers in Australia took an ale culture with them from Britain and Ireland. Lager arrived in the late 19th century thanks to the Foster brothers from New York who briefly cornered the market in bottom-fermented beers due to their ownership of a refrigeration plant. They returned to the US but left behind a name that became a world brewing giant. Other brewers rushed to produce lagers heavily dosed with local cane sugar. But despite the awesome domination today of Castlemaine and Foster's, a few ales and even a few stouts have survived, and one ale in particular has become a cult drink.

Cascade Premium Lager

Cascade is the oldest continuously working brewery in Australia. The superb red-brick plant looks like a cross between a traditional English brewery and a Yorkshire woollen mill. It was opened in 1832 to brew ale and porter and was owned by Peter Desgraves from Dover in England who designed the brewery, Hobart's theatre and the saw mill while he was serving time for bankruptcy.

Tasmania is a major barley-growing area and supplies most of Australia's hops, including the Pride of Ringwood variety which may have originated in Hampshire, England. The brewery is named after the Cascade mountains, the source of its pure brewing water. It merged

with the island's other brewery, Boag, in 1922, and switched to lager production in 1927. Premium Lager (5.2 per cent abv) is a noticeably full-bodied beer by Australian lager standards with a crisp finish and some citric hop notes. The brewery also produces Draught, Bitter and Stout, all bottom fermented despite their names. The stout has plenty of roasted malt and chocolate character.

Cascade Brewery Company, 156 Collins Street, Hobart, Tasmania 7000.

COOPER'S SPARKLING ALE AND STOUT

At the height of the lager boom, one company went on brewing ale to the general derision of the rest of the brewing industry. But today Cooper's Sparkling Ale from Adelaide is a cult beer in Australia and is recognised worldwide as a classic. Thomas Cooper emigrated from Yorkshire in 1825. His wife was an innkeeper's daughter and she used her brewing skills to make beer at home. Thomas gave up his day job to concentrate on brewing. His descendants still run the company. They have remained faithful to ale and didn't add a lager to their portfolio until 1969. The 5.8 per cent abv Sparkling Ale is bottle conditioned and throws a heavy yeast sediment after six weeks' conditioning in the brewery. The title "sparkling" causes some amusement as the beer tends to be cloudy in the glass. It is brewed from pale and crystal malts, with cane sugar making up around 18 per cent of the recipe. Hops are Pride of Ringwood and bitterness units are 26. After primary fermentation, the beer is given a dosage of fermenting wort and sugar. This encourages a strong secondary fermentation. Sparkling Ale is intensely fruity, with apple and banana dominating, a peppery hop aroma, citric fruit in the mouth, and a quenching finish with more hops and fruit. Cooper's Stout (6.8 per cent) is also bottle conditioned, with roasted malt added to pale

Opposite
Thomas Cooper came from Yorkshire and founded a brewing dynasty.
Above
Sparkling Ale and Stout are classics that have bucked the trend to pale, sweetish lagers.

Below
Redback is a bottle-conditioned wheat beer named after a venomous spider.
Opposite
Foster's, world-famous for its lager brand, has remained true to tradition with a top-fermenting stout.

and crystal. It has an oily, coffeeish aroma and palate and a dry, chocolatey finish with a good balance of hops.
Cooper's Brewery, 9 Statenborough Street, Leabrook, Adelaide, South Australia 5068.

Redback Wheat Beer

Matilda Bay was set up by Philip Sexton, a brewer formerly with Swan. In 1984, he built a brewpub, the Sail and Anchor, in Fremantle and later added his Matilda Bay micro plant. With capital from Foster's, he has also opened a sizeable brewery in Perth. His main brand, Redback (named after a local spider) was the first Australian wheat beer. Made from 65 per cent malted wheat, with two-row barley malt using Hersbrücker and Saaz hops, the 4.8 per cent abv bottle-conditioned beer has 18 units of bitterness. The yeast strain was imported from Bavaria. It has an apple-fruit aroma and palate, with more tart fruit and spices in the finish. It is refreshing in a hot climate. An "ale" called Dogbolter is bottom fermented. The Sail and Anchor specializes in handpumped, English-style ales.
Matilda Bay Brewing Company, 130 Stirling Highway, North Fremantle, Western Australia 6159.

SHEAF STOUT

Carlton & United Breweries is part of the giant Foster's group. A genuine, top-fermenting stout came its way with the acquisition of Tooth's Brewery in Sydney, founded by John Tooth from Kent, in England, who used the old hop-sack insiginia of the White Horse of Kent on his labels. Sheaf Stout (5.7 per cent abv, with 35 units of bitterness) is brewed from pale and crystal malts with some roasted barley. It is jet-black in colour with a woody aroma from the grain and possibly the hops, an espresso coffee palate, and hops, dark fruit and liquorice in the finish.

CUB has also continued to produce Tooth's Kent Old Brown, a top-fermenting amber ale not unlike the famous brown ales of North-east England. Foster's great rival, Castlemaine Perkins, has also kept going a stout called Carbine, named after a famous racehorse, but it is now bottom fermenting.

Carlton & United Breweries, 26 Broadway, Sydney, New South Wales 2000.

Index